Democracy and Poetry

The 1974 Jefferson Lecture in the Humanities

And it is enough for the poet
  to be the guilty conscience of his time.

—St.-John Perse

Democracy and Poetry

Robert Penn Warren

Harvard University Press

Cambridge, Massachusetts
and
London, England
1975

Copyright © 1975 by Robert Penn Warren
All rights reserved
Library of Congress Catalog Card Number 74-31993
ISBN 0-674-19625-2
Printed in the United States of America

To
Andrew Nelson Lytle
and the memory of
Edna Barker Lytle

Acknowledgments

I am deeply indebted to the National Foundation for the Humanities, under whose auspices these remarks were first presented, as the Jefferson Lecture of 1974, and in a more direct and personal way to Ronald Berman and Robert J. Kingston for their many kindnesses. I take great pleasure also in remembering the combination of good heart and hard editorial eye that I have enjoyed and profited from in Ann Louise Coffin McLaughlin and Aida DiPace Donald of the Harvard University Press.

Fairfield, Connecticut   R.P.W.
February 16, 1975

Contents

Foreword

SINCE THE disproportion between these essays may strike some readers as odd, I should, perhaps, offer an explanation. In working toward the Jefferson lectures, I wrote a mass of notes to myself as well as a continuous discussion. I worked from that mass and finally came out with two related discussions tailored to the accustomed fifty-five minutes—10,000 words in all. But in tidying up the actual lectures for publication, I found that, for illustration and clarification, I was drawing on my original reservoir of ideas and formulations as well as adding new ones. For better or worse, that was the process of revision, and one of its results is the lengthy second essay.

The concern of the discussion that follows is the interrelation of three things: democracy, poetry (really art in general), and selfhood. Each of these terms, of necessity, leads through a brambly tangle of definitions. Yet, though I recognized that the problem was serious, I did not begin by trying to frame them, hoping that along the way definitions adequate to the occasion would emerge. For the term democracy this was worked out well enough, I trust. How could anyone miss the issues involved in this big, overshadowing problem of our age? As for poetry, some readers may quite properly object that I reveal myself as parochially of the Western world. This is all too true; but after all, it is with that Western world that we are here primarily concerned, and, again, the definition implied in the discussion may be adequate for the occasion.

When it comes to the notion of self, however, the situation is somewhat different. As we live from day to day, our sense of personal identity seems to require no explanation. We simply "live" our selfhood. But the concept of self, once scrutinized, is, as I am at least partially aware, enormously complex and problematical. A testimony to this fact is the massive literature on the subject that extends from the early days of the Greek and Hebraic worlds to the most recent article on "quickie" psychology or handbook on self-help. And I am also aware, even in my slender acquaintance with that literature, that there is no easy and ready orthodoxy. Since there is none, it may be useful, even at this date, to provide the reader with a guiding statement as to what I mean by the self: in individuation, the felt principle of significant unity.

The qualifiers felt and significant demand special comment. By *felt* I mean that I am here concerned, not with a theoretical analysis as such, but with what a more or less aware individual may experience as his own self-hood, and what he assumes about other individuals. By *significant* I mean two things: continuity—the self as a development in time, with a past and a future; and responsibility—the self as a moral identity, recognizing itself as capable of action worthy of praise or blame.

A reader may object that I am here dealing with qualities only sometimes achieved by a self, by an individuated, separate entity. I fully realize that most of us only partially achieve a self of the sort I describe; nevertheless, I must stand on my notions, for I cannot see how a self otherwise conceived can be relevant to either democracy or poetry.

In essays such as these, behind almost every paragraph lies some unargued assumption which may be objected to. Of some of these assumptions I am aware, but undoubtedly there are some of which I am not aware. All I can hope, for both the conscious and the unconscious assumptions, is that, even if they are not acceptable to a reader, they may exhibit some sort of coherence, some internal consistency.

One of my assumptions is so important for my line of thought that I should try to bring it into the open. Let us approach it in the form of the following objection: "You talk as though there is some necessary connection between poetry and democracy. But what of great poetry—great art—created in periods or under regimes that were anti-democratic?"

My answer would run something like this. We cannot discuss democracy or poetry as existing outside of history, as a matter of timeless, unconditioned options. They, like all things that we esteem or abhor, represent developments in time. As for democracy, looking back over history, over a preindustrial world, we can scarcely conceive of the development of civilization without mass labor, often brutalizing and miserable, as the economic base to support an elite of some sort. In such societies, however much the notion may offend our moral sensibilities, we recognize that the slave, the helot, the villein, the serf, the peasant, the untouchable was not regarded as a person at all.

The poetry of such a elite order did, however, develop the conception of selfhood. When the Greeks hit upon the notion of man as the measure of all things, they hit, as a corollary, upon the notion of the self as the central fact of "poetry." The notion was, in its manifestations, aristocratic, even heroic. Gods and goddesses, kings and queens, heroes and heroines populate the narrative of Homer, but we recognize them now as human "selves" of great variety and depth. Sophocles, no more than Homer, arose in what we would call a democratic society, but the figure of Oedipus, in his buskins taller than life and uttering grandly through the hieratic mask, exhibited the struggles of a self trapped in the anguish of its fate. ·

What I am getting at here is that the concept of self, with the associated values and issues, was central to poetry, and that the concept, in the turn of time, though in an imperfect, stumbling, and ragged way, was to become more and more widely available to men. In the turn of time, every man might become a king, or at least a hero. Such poetry, however, did not advertise only the aristocratic virtue; it advertised tenderness, too, as in the scene of Hector's farewell to Andromache and his infant son, who is frightened by the great crest of the warrior's helmet and must be comforted. Tenderness, too, was to become more widely available: every man might become a man.

For a parallel here we may think of the "democracy" of fifth-century Athens or that of the Roman Republic. There was in neither case a democracy that we would recognize as such, merely a democracy of aristocrats, and the growth of the idea of the self in such a context is a parallel to the process of political development; as Marx puts it in *The Eighteenth Brumaire*, the "Roman class struggle was only fought out within a privileged minority." But the concept of the citizen embodied in those societies was eventually to become more and more available, and a vision of Athens and Rome hung in the air for Jefferson as he penned the Declaration. Or, to take another parallel: the world that nourished the Stoic philosophy was even less democratic than fifth-century Athens or the Roman Republic, but that philosophy has, over centuries, nourished the expanding notion of the self. And if Christianity is to be regarded as a great central force in developing the notion of the significance of the self, and of democracy, what are we to make of all the paradoxes found in its history?

To return to poetry, we have been speaking of the content, but as a sort of footnote, I suggest that the poetic act, whatever the content, represents an assertion of the self. What is at stake here will, I trust, emerge later.

It will likely occur to some readers that there is something self-justifying and even defensive in these essays; that they represent the old, recurring reflex of arts and letters against the "real" world. That may be true. Certainly what I have written here may be better taken as "meditations" than "essays." Whatever they may be called, they do represent, in some degree, an utterance of a rather personal sort, a personal exploration, if you will. For all of my adult years, my central and obsessive concern has been with "poetry," and I scarcely find it strange that I should seek some connection between that concern and the "real" world.

Who wants to be a superfluous man? Unless, of course, he feels that his superfluousness is a mark of spiritual superiority—a proof that he is of finer clay?

West Wardsboro, Vermont   R. P. W.

America and the Diminished Self

LET ME EXPLAIN as briefly as possible what I hope to do in this essay. But first I should say that I mean the word *poetry* in the broad sense of all the "making" which is art. As for my general aim, it is to explore the necessary connection between poetry and our basic notion of democracy—American democracy. I review our "poetry" here as a criticism—often a corrosive criticism—of our actual achievements over the years in democracy. The central point of the review is that the decay of the concept of self has been, consciously or unconsciously, a developing and fundamental theme of our writers, and I try to indicate some connection between that fact and the course of our general history. In the second essay I endeavor to document the decay of the concept of self in relation to our present society and its ideals. But my emphasis there turns from the diagnostic role of "poetry" to its therapeutic role.

3

So with this little chart, and with a skipper about whose seamanship the less said the better, we embark on the tumultuous seas of our history.

Thomas Jefferson, in whose honor these meditations are offered, never applied the word *democrat* to himself, nor does the word *democracy* appear in the Declaration of Independence. In that time the word was, in fact, almost synonymous with riot and anarchy. But Jefferson did envisage a society in which free men—of independent self—would exercise their franchise in the light of reason.

The dream of Jefferson, the aristocrat, the scion of the Enlightenment, was to assume, some eighty years after he had penned his Declaration, a new formulation at the hands of a plebian son of Romanticism, who was a homosexual mystic. Jefferson might have recognized certain ideas in Whitman's formulation as continuators of his own, but he, as a social man, in the eighteenth-century sense, would probably have been befuddled by the tone of the opening lines of "Song of Myself":

I celebrate myself, and sing myself,
And what I assume you shall assume,
For every atom belonging to me as good belong to you.

And Jefferson would have been equally befuddled when Whitman, in "Long, Too Long America," demanded of America:

For who except myself has yet conceiv'd what
your children en-masse really are?

But well before Whitman's first hymning of himself
and of America as somehow forming a mystic unity, the
political system of the Founding Fathers had been
democratized, with universal manhood suffrage ("uni-
versal" meaning white, of course), and with the "tumul-
tuous populace of large cities," which Washington had
declared is always to be "dreaded," now multiplied
manyfold. The Jeffersonian dream had assumed the
shape of what, to many Americans, was the Jacksonian
nightmare. The most famous report of the nightmare
shape may be the following quotation from Emerson:

Leave this hypocritical prating about the masses.
Masses are rude, lame, unmade, pernicious in their
demands and influence . . . I wish not to concede
anything to them, but to tame, drill, divide, and break
them up, and draw individuals out of them . . . I do
not wish any mass at all, but honest men only . . .
and no shovel-handed, narrow-brained, gin-drinking
million stockingers or lazzaroni at all . . . Away with
this hurrah of masses, and let us have the considered
vote of single men spoken on their honor and their
conscience.

But Emerson and Whitman, for all differences be-
tween them, were still Jeffersonians. If Emerson berated

his fellow-citizens for accepting a democracy of shovel-handed, gin-drinking lazzaroni, what he wanted was to have the "considered vote of single men spoken on their honor and their conscience." In other words, Emerson did have some hope for a democracy of responsible individuals, of selves, to be drawn from the masses— even if he, bemused in his Neoplatonism and rapt, to borrow the phrase which Keats applied to Wordsworth, in the "egotistical sublime," was sometimes not quite sure of the reality of the objective world.

Certain other democrats had views different from those of Emerson and Whitman. James Fenimore Cooper, who declared himself a democrat, was one, we may say, *faute de mieux.* Cooper, after observing the various "defective systems of government of the human race," was "far from saying," as he put it, "that our own, with all its flagrant and obvious defects, will be the worst." The defects he observed, like those noted by Tocqueville, were lack of standards of taste and conduct, a craven conformity to popular prejudice, a contempt for, para-doxically, both individual dignity and the social good, the tyranny of majority rule, the corrupting influence of plutocracy, and the rape of, and alienation from, nature. Plutocracy would strike, he said, at the very roots of democracy by the use of demagogic perversions of the language of democracy, and by the press that, "as soon as the money-getting principle is applied to it," would convert facts "into articles for the market." It is Cooper's hatred of plutocracy that informs the characters Hutter and Hurry Harry in *The Deerslayer*. Hutter is an ex-pirate now driven inland to hole up on Lake Glimmerglas and Hurry Harry is, as the name suggests, a frontier exemplar of the go-getter. It is this pair who try to persuade the young Leatherstocking to raid an unprotected Indian camp to take scalps from the women and children for the bounty money that white law would pay. So piracy and go-getterism go hand in hand.

As for the rape of nature and the alienation of man from nature, the theme is nowhere better dramatized than in *The Pioneers*, in which, on the one hand, the aged Natty Bumppo, who kills only for meat, is tried for violating the newfangled game law, while, on the other hand, the entire village turns out, even with a cannon, for the wanton slaughter of a vast flock of passenger pigeons. This theme is a central concern of the Leatherstocking saga, and Natty Bumppo himself is a complex embodiment of it; he mediates between the pole of nature and that of civilization, between that of natural freedom and that of law, between that of reverence for nature and that of the use of nature. Leatherstocking is, we may say, the mythical image of the perfect democrat, morally self-disciplined to respect both nature and man—in a sense the mythic projection of the virtues of the "democratic gentleman," which Cooper takes to provide the standards of society. For Cooper, his special brand of democrat, whether Leatherstocking or the "gentleman," was most clearly a "self"—more clearly, freestandingly, and magnanimously a "self" than even

Jefferson, Emerson, or Whitman dared to dream. And all of Cooper's criticisms of democracy are directed to the end of making, insofar as is possible in a fallen world, a democracy of "selves."

Somehow, with whatever fragility, the Jeffersonian dream, based on the assumption of a responsible self, did survive the actualities of American life. The dream survived even the enemies it carried in its own womb, creatures as diverse as Hutter the ex-pirate and Hurry Harry the go-getter at one end of the spectrum, and Henry David Thoreau at the other—Thoreau, who struck at the root of the democratic process when he declared that "any man more right than his neighbors constitutes a majority of one," and even at the root of all society when he declared to the world that he wanted no part of its "dirty institutions." The Jeffersonian dream not only survived, but with the Civil War and the apotheosis of Lincoln in martyrdom, seemed to find vindication in actuality—the common man perfected in artistic sensibility, folk humor, courage, compassion, and humility—the self perfected in selflessness.

But something went wrong. Melville was the first American writer to sniff the dead rat behind the baseboard. He, one of the old breed of giants from before the flood, had dreamed the heroic lineaments of Ahab etched against a lightning-split firmament. But now, though a good Unionist, Melville harbored the unhappy suspicion that the Civil War might have deeper and more ambiguous meanings than officially appeared. In the poem "The

Conflict of Convictions," in *Battle-Pieces* (1866), his poetic interpretation of the war, Melville predicted that with the victory of federal arms and of "Right,"

> Power unanointed may come—
> Dominion (unsought by the free)
> And the Iron Dome,
> Stronger for stress and strain,
> Fling her huge shadow athwart the main;
> But the Founders' dream shall flee.

History, in other words, "spins against the way it drives." Even Whitman was beginning to find this out, for a few years later, in *Democratic Vistas*, he could ask if, in the victorious North, there were now, "indeed men . . . worthy of the name." And his answer was that he found only a "sort of dry and flat Sahara" and cities "crowded with petty grotesques, malformations, phantoms, playing meaningless antics."

Already, before Melville's poem, the very young Henry Adams, a secretary to his father, the wartime minister at the Court of Saint James's, had written, "my philosophy teaches me . . . that the laws which govern animated beings will be ultimately found to be at bottom the same with those that rule inanimate matter." Even with this strictly naturalistic philosophy, the young Adams could assert his belief that the "great principle of democracy is still capable of rewarding a conscientious servant"; and after the war, as late as 1868, he could come to Washington to set up as a philosophic critic and mentor for virtue in the midst of the political hurly-burly.

But the world, presumably driven by those forces that rule animate as well as inanimate matter, swept on its way, leaving him to teach medieval history at Harvard and then write his novel *Democracy* (1880). In the novel, the Lincolnesque Senator Silas P. Ratcliffe, the "Prairie Giant of Peonia, the Favorite Son of Illinois," generally taken to be the embodiment of democratic virtue, is revealed as a crook, and the heroine, an idealistic lady who, like the young Adams, had come to Washington to validate her hope for her country, and who is on the verge of marrying the Senator, must ruefully admit that democracy has "shaken" her "nerves to pieces." And here we note that corruption is spawned not in the slums of the great cities that George Washington had feared, but comes, in the mask of Lincoln, from the heartland of America and the class that Jefferson had assumed to represent the core of the democratic faith.

Historical determinism, positivism, Darwinism, pragmatism, Marxism—it was an age of new "isms," and all of them, reasonably or unreasonably, in a sophisticated or vulgar form, called into question the old romantic mystique of democracy. Obviously, something had happened when, in the belief of the young soldier Holmes in general laws of nature, we see implicit his later notions that "all life is an experiment" and man only a "cosmic ganglion" and a "predatory animal," and that "society rests on the death of men." This did not mean that

Holmes, in spite of being an excessively self-conscious aristocrat ("I loathe the thick-fingered clowns we call the people," he early wrote, and never seems to have changed his mind), was not a good and faithful servant of democracy—even if he did serve with his own not-thick philosophical fingers crossed. Democracy was not for him a divine, or even a historical, revelation. For him it was, as for Cooper and Melville, simply a social and political arrangement, not a mystique—ultimately a gamble.* Once this has been said, the old religious devotion to democracy is undercut, and Jefferson and Whitman seem strangely callow, along with Lincoln, to whom, according to Alexander Stephens, Vice President of the Confederacy, the Union, that embodiment of democracy, had risen to the sublimity of religious mysticism. If Melville greatly admired Lincoln, as he indeed did, it was not because of this fact.

Now this is not to say that a pragmatist (and this is what Holmes and even, in one dimension, Melville, along with William James, were) may not have a patriot's devotion. It is, however, to say that such devotion to a mere arrangement, a gamble, an experiment, is likely to be caviar to the general. It is not what you tell the sixth-grade civics class or the electorate.

*Historians have pointed out that the Founding Fathers frequently used the word *experiment* in reference to the new government they sought to establish, as when Madison called it the "experiment of an extended republic." But there was a difference here from what is meant by Holmes. Madison, Adams, Franklin, et al., were simply referring to the practicality of the mechanism they were trying to contrive; they had little doubt about the values they aimed at. Holmes's skepticism involved values: the "good" depends on the "municipal jurisdiction."

11

For all the differences between the philosophers and "the general," they all sprang from the same seedbed. Some of the same elements in the American experience that had led to the new philosophy of speculative men like Adams, Holmes, and William James, had led, too, to the new kind of behavior in men of action. After the war, when Charles Francis Adams, the younger, the brother of Henry, got back from battle and settled into civilian life, he remarked of the new breed:

> The great operations of war, the handling of large masses of men, the influence of discipline, the lavish expenditures of unprecedented.sums of money, the immense financial operations, the possibilities of effective cooperation were lessons not likely to be lost on men quick to receive and to apply all new ideas.

The lessons were not lost, and by 1879, William H. Vanderbilt (the son of the old Commodore), testifying before the Hepburn Committee in regard to railroad rates and discrimination, described his contemporaries:

> You can't keep such men down . . . I don't believe that by any legislative enactment or anything else through any of the States or all of the States, you can keep such men down. You can't do it.

So here we have the young Henry Adams' theory that "the laws that govern animated beings" are the same, and equally as amoral, as "those that rule inanimate matter." And have, too, an example of Melville's notion that history may spin against the way it drives—may, that is, in the "spin" give a war for freedom, and in the "drive" a war to create Jim Fisk, the "Skunk of Wall Street." And remotely over the scene we may envision the appalled face of Emerson, who, in one of his more striking paradoxes, had declared: "Money . . . is in its effects and laws as beautiful as roses. Property keeps the accounts of the world and is always moral." The declaration had come true in a way the Sage of Concord could scarcely have envisaged, and was to be paraphrased, as a summarizing philosophy of the Age of the Robber Barons, by Bishop Lawrence of Massachusetts: "Godliness is in league with riches . . . Material prosperity is helping to make the national character sweeter, more joyous, more unselfish, more Christlike."

So the Emersonian self suffered a transformation: into Hurry Harry as vestryman.

I have touched on such figures as Adams, William James, Holmes, Vanderbilt, and Bishop Lawrence, none of whom is a poet even by the utmost wrenching of the term, because in their various ways they represent the atmosphere which the "poets," the "makers," of the time did breathe. As for such "makers" as Henry James and William Dean Howells, they are much to our purpose of showing the shift in feeling of writers toward their country. James's life embodied profound and tangled ambivalences about America, and actually he would have agreed with Hawthorne's remark that "the United States are fit for many excellent purposes, but they are certainly not fit to live in." If this remark, in a letter to W. D. Tichnor, from Rome in 1858, when Hawthorne* was brooding on his country as it slid

*The importance of Hawthorne to my line of thought here is great, but indirect. Hawthorne could not well imagine the relation of a self to a community beyond a certain physical scale; a community, to be real to him, had to be more or less immediately graspable, and he thought in such terms rather than in abstractions such as "shared values" or an "ethos." For instance, though he could say, in a rather fleeting mood provoked by the coming of the Civil War, that it was "delightful . . . to feel I had a country," we find in the same letter that Americans "never really had a country" (letter to Horation Bridge, May 26, 1861, in Horation Bridge, *Personal Recollections of Nathaniel Hawthorne*, New York, 1893, pp. 168–170). And a little earlier there is the following entry in his *Journal*: "I wonder that we in America love our country at all, it having no limits . . . when you try to make it a matter of heart, everything falls away except one's native state; neither can you seize hold of that unless you tear it out of the Union, bleeding and quivering" (entry of October 11, 1858, in Newton Arvin, ed., *The Heart of Hawthorne's Journals*, Cambridge, Mass., 1929). Hawthorne was at the opposite end of the spectrum from Whitman, who hymned a massive America with its children "en masse."

As for Hawthorne's fiction, a fundamental concern is with the depth and paradoxicality of human motives, that is, with the complexity of the self and not with its attenuation, which is our present topic. But in some of his fiction, most notably *The Scarlet Letter*, the drama does involve the development of a self in relation to a community, a development depending on a dialectic between shared values and tensions. In any case, it is certainly logical to think that with the transformation of community, as Hawthorne conceived it, into the massive society, Whitmanian or technological, he would have feared the maiming of the self. It may even be relevant here, in connection with Hawthorne's complex psychological and moral obsessions, to quote from Erik Erikson: "could it be that our special [modern] curiosity concerning unconscious motivation is itself a further development of an evolutionary need for an ever-more conscious core of self-sameness in the acceleration of technological and scientific change?" (*Dimensions of a New Identity*, New York, 1974, p. 101). If the philosophy and social views of the Transcendentalists were in reaction to the rise of the infant industrial order toward civil war, represented only a mood, it would for James represent a settled conviction on which he acted.

The case of Howells is more dramatic. For years he was a staunch Republican who, as a young man on the make, had written the campaign biography for Lincoln; and years later, when Cleveland became the first Democratic President after 1860, he could mourn: "A great cycle has come to a close; the rule of the best in politics for a quarter of a century is ended."

Clearly, Howells' party loyalty knew no bounds; but something was going on in the deeper recesses of his being, and soon he was to write *The Rise of Silas Lapham*, a story of American success, and was reading Tolstoi— two not unrelated events that were to lead to his sudden vision of the degradation and misery within the shell of the new plutocracy that had proved so kind to the boy from Jefferson, Ohio. Howells even considered taking penitential refuge in some village to lead the life of a Tolstoian peasant.

It is, however, Mark Twain who most deeply embodied the tensions of his time, even though he may have been less aware than Howells of the implications of his own inner drama, or even less aware than Balzac was of how the meaning of the massive and intricate world he created ran in opposition to his own political views and social aspirations. As Harold Rosenberg has

---

and mass society, then we may find, according to Erikson's reasoning, a parallel reaction, differently targeted of course, in the special inwardness of Hawthorne's fiction.

remarked, "the decision to be revolutionary [now a fashion] counts for very little," for "the most radical changes have come from personalities who were conservative." Rosenberg was referring to revolution in art, but it is equally true that the role of the writer may betray the man who happens to be a writer into a logic of imagination that undercuts his ideology and his personal ambitions. To reverse the famous formula of Yeats, poetry may not merely spring from the quarrel with the self, but may expose (or even create) the quarrel. To regard the matter in a somewhat different perspective, the artist may be regarded as a man who cannot project outside himself the "shadow" self, but must live with it.

In any case, there must have been unresolvable tensions in a man who, in his last coma, talked of Dr. Jekyll and Mr. Hyde; and Mark Twain's relation to the issues of his age is full of extraordinary ambivalences. For instance, he repudiated the historical past (including his father and the South), but the telling and retelling of his personal past, directly or indirectly, became his chief stock-in-trade. Then, in this telling of the personal past, emerged new ambivalences and new tangles. He knew, to take an example, the worst about Hannibal, Missouri, the poverty, violence, and despair; and to a boyhood friend of Hannibal days, who looked back nostalgically to the lost time, he wrote:

As to the past, there is but one good thing about it
. . . that it is the past . . . I can see by your manner
of speech, that for more than twenty years you have
stood dead still in the midst of the dreaminess, the
melancholy, the romance, the heroics, of sweet but
sappy sixteen. Man, do you know that this is simply
mental and moral masturbation?

This sounds very explicit, but the divided mind of
Twain is indicated by the fact that this no-nonsense
utterance occurs in 1876, the very year when he was
publishing *The Adventures of Tom Sawyer*, which, in a very
different mood, he called "simply a hymn, put into prose
to give it a worldly air." It was indeed a hymn to boy-
hood and innocence; but Twain's dream of innocence
took many disguises. There was the vision of moonlight
on the Mississippi as seen from the texas deck of a
steamboat, where the pilot reigned in lonely glory. The
dream of innocence could appear, too, in his image of
himself as above the prevalent lust for Grab; for
instance, when he described himself as "not much fired
with a mania for money-getting." Or he might strike
forth in righteous anger against the corruption of the
age, as in a public letter to Vanderbilt after one of the
Commodore's more outrageous exploits: "All I wish to
urge you now is that you crush out your native instincts
and do something worthy of praise . . . Go boldly,
proudly, nobly, and give four dollars to some worthy
charity." Yet all the while Twain's own passion for

wealth and the company of nabobs went undiminished. Obsessed with the Paige typesetting machine, he bent every effort to become a nabob himself; until bankruptcy snapped that hope and he had to be rescued by one H. H. Rogers of the Standard Oil Company. But he still nourished such schemes; even at the time when, in "The Man Who Corrupted Hadleyburg," he was exhibiting the moral consequences of the American dream of quick and stupendous wealth.

The ambivalences, the tensions, were central to Twain's being, but in his most famous book, *Adventures of Huckleberry Finn*, one of the impulses seems to have been to resolve them. The basic conflict in the novel is, of course, between the life on the river, where Huck finds innocence, brotherhood with man, and communion with nature, and life ashore, where, stage by stage, he discovers the corruption of society, a process that comes to climax when conscience itself is exhibited as the creature of society, embodying its most cruel mandates. As Huck gradually develops a new "consciousness" to replace the old "conscience," the reader's expectation rises that Huck may find for himself—and for the reader—a way to redeem life ashore, to create a life in which the "real" of the shore and the "ideal" of the river may meet, or at least enter into some fruitful relation.

But nothing of the sort occurs. At the end, Huck finds himself conniving in the famously brutal joke, at Nigger Jim's expense, that undercuts all the moral discovery on the river. To cap the climax, he finds himself caught in the very trap of society from which he had sought escape on the river, with his only comfort now in the vague notion that he may cut out for the "territory"— even though Twain well knew what the "territory" would become in the course of winning the West. So we are left with the irremediable split—and presumably an unredeemable world and a self that, as long as it is of that world, is unredeemable, too.

It is *A Connecticut Yankee at King Arthur's Court* that most nakedly exhibits the unresolvable issues that had lain behind the struggle to complete the earlier novel. Now when Twain began *A Connecticut Yankee* he had in mind little more than a savage joke at the expense of the romantic cult of medievalism and more indirectly at the expense, probably, of the late Confederate States, under whose flag Samuel Clemens had briefly and ineffectually borne arms. But soon, to the savage jest at the expense of the past, there was joined, not a "hymn" to boyhood and innocence, but a "hymn" to modernity.

Hank Morgan, a superintendent at the Colt Arms Company, who in his technician's pride asserts that he can "invent, contrive, create" anything, sets out to introduce the natives of Arthurian Britain, in which he mysteriously finds himself, to the blessings of technological civilization. This mission of humanitarian improvement goes hand in glove, however, with Hank's program to become the "Boss"; that is, in an unconscious parody of imperialism and strange forerunner of Conrad's *Heart of Darkness* the role of humane civilizer

19

and that of the exploiter merge. Or, to leap from the Belgian Congo of the late nineteenth century to the Western world of the late twentieth, the establishing of a rational order demands centralized authority, and ironically the effort to free man may end in a new form of tyranny.

In any case, Hank becomes the Boss, surrounded by a corps of young Janizaries devoted to technology and to him. In the last battle against the forces of darkness clad in clanking armor, he unveils his masterpiece of inventiveness and human liberation, and his mines fill the air with "a steady drizzle of microscopic fragments of knights and hardware and horseflesh"—to use the phrase Hank Morgan applies to an earlier exploit with a simple dynamite bomb. So, with this drizzle the myth of progress and the hymn to redemptive modernity wind up with the Boss and his Janizaries victorious but fatally imprisoned by ramparts of the putrescent dead. They wind up with Hank sunk in a cynical contempt for what he now calls "human muck," the very people he had hoped to redeem by reason and technology; and with the phrase "human muck" we find the death knell of the faith in the common sense of the common man. As for Hank himself, he is left, when translated back to his proper century, with a hatred of life lightened only, in a last delirium, by a wistful backward look on the love of his wife Sandy, in the midst of the beauty of the green world of Britain before he had blessed it with the victory of modernity at the battle of the Sand Belt.

In the course of writing his book, the joke on the past had backfired on Twain to become a joke on the future. When the book was finished, he wrote of it to Howells: "if it were only to write over again," it "would require . . . a pen warmed up in hell."

If *A Connecticut Yankee* is fraught with dire forebodings about democracy in general and, more appallingly, about modern .industrial-technological democracy in particular, that grimness is as nothing compared to what was to come, after our Philippine operetta of imperialism, in "To a Person Sitting in Darkness." Or in this passage from "Papers of the Adam Family":

> But it was impossible to save the Great Republic. She was rotten to the heart. Lust of conquest had long since done its work; trampling upon the helpless abroad had taught her, by a natural process, to endure with apathy the like at home . . . The government was irrevocably in the hands of the prodigiously rich and their hangers-on; the suffrage was to become a mere machine . . . There was no principle but commercialism, no patriotism but of the pocket.

To compound this gloomy prophecy for American democracy, Twain had come to agree with Hank that the human race was "muck." Or if not muck, it was wicked vermin, as in *The Mysterious Stranger*, where Satan, who, to please the boy Theodor, having molded and vitalized some little creatures of clay, picks up a couple who had got to fighting and with his fingers crushes them and flings the miniscule bodies aside and then wipes away the blood smear on his handkerchief—meanwhile pursuing his conversation. Man's infinite capacity for folly and infinite capacity for wickedness, in the face of all his shabby pretenses, is Twain's final theme, and the fact that American democracy is, by his standards, one of the shabbier pretensions gets almost forgotten.

No, this is not Twain's final theme. The final theme even more drastically undercuts the whole concept of a democratic—or any other kind of—social order, and therefore renders irrelevant any criticism of, or hope for, man. All is illusion, a "fever-dream." As he writes his sister-in-law Sue Crane:

> I dreamed I was born and grew up and was a pilot on the Mississippi and a miner and a journalist in Nevada and a pilgrim in the *Quaker City*, and had a wife and children and went to live in a villa at Florence—and this dream goes on and on and sometimes seems so real that I almost believe it is real.

If nothing is real, there is no guilt. And there are no problems of politics, society, justice, or history. Except those of spooks. Who, of course, have no "self" to cast a vote "spoken on their honor and their conscience."

At the very moment when Twain had his first success, Theodore Dreiser was born, in 1871. Dreiser, with almost schematic precision, embodied in his life, and dramatized in his work, the same issues that obsessed Twain, but brought them forward into the terms of our century. Dreiser was a child of the Gilded Age who, unlike Twain, had no happy recollection of boyhood in the old agrarian America, however mythical. Dreiser was not only the son of poverty and failure, but also the son of an immigrant with the immigrant's psychology. He was the born outsider, the born yearner, ugly, uncouth, and poorly educated, the ferocious masturbator dreaming of some girl both beautiful and rich, incapable of love, fearful of impotence but a ruthless womanizer, a self-absorbed and ambitious believer in a reductive social Darwinism who, nevertheless, was a moralist—and a genius.

The work of this genius revolved around two related themes, the central themes of his age: the nature of success and the nature of the self. Sister Carrie of his first novel is, as he calls her, "a little soldier of fortune," the ignorant farm girl with no education and no firm principle, who comes to the new booming Chicago and ends as a famous actress in New York. Sex is her weapon, but she is, as Kenneth Lynn has pointed out, the classic example of the golddigger to whom sex means little or nothing in itself. Furthermore, she has the most meager talent. She simply stumbles into a society that demands nothing of her except that she be precisely what she is. The story is, in general, about success as a mechanical process and, in the end, about the blankness of success. We last see Carrie, sitting in her rich apartment in the Waldorf, with a copy of *Le Père Goriot* on her knee. And Balzac's novel, we remember, is the story of another *arriviste*, whose career, like hers, is as amoral as a chemical experiment. Here the Horatio Alger story, beloved of every red-blooded American boy, is turned upside down.

In Dreiser's massive work on American business, *The Trilogy of Desire* (which includes *The Financier* and *The Titan*) the name of the hero carries, too, an ironical echo of the Alger myth—Frank Algernon Cowperwood: Algernon = not Alger. But Cowperwood, except for the fact of success, has scarcely anything in common with honest little Horatio. Cowperwood's notion of honesty, to begin with, is purely relative, and to take a phrase from Justice Holmes's sardonic definition of "right," is dependent only on the "municipal jurisdiction." True, Cowperwood does do a hitch in the pen, but that is, in his society and in his own mind, little more than an industrial accident, and does not impede his world-shaking success. His honesty, after all, is appropriate to the "municipal jurisdiction" in which he operates, that is, post-Civil War America.

Cowperwood differs, moreover, from the little Horatio who reverences womanhood, and especially American womanhood. Cowperwood is the ruthless womanizer, with a blue stare, as blazing as a Bunsen burner, and no female can withstand it. Cowperwood collects not only women but art as well, and oddly enough both art and women represent some very un-Horatio-like spiritual yearnings, never to be gratified. And this leads to the paradox in Cowperwood.

Cowperwood is a philosopher and his philosophy is a social Darwinism as amoral as the goings-on in a jungle, a philosophy that he sums up with the motto, "I please myself." The paradox is that, by pleasing himself, he, the superman, has no self. He is, as Dreiser finally describes him, a prince of dreams, the victim of illusion, and the last illusion is that of the self. What his blazing and unfulfilled career "demonstrates" is "the wonder and terror of individuality."

Of "individuality"—but we may substitute the word *individualism* and we have, then, by extension, the proposition that the prime example of individualism, the man of will who says "I please myself," is the victim of the last illusion: he can have no self. Why? Because the true self, among the many varieties of fictive selves, can develop only in a vital relation between the unitary person and the group. That is, the self is possible only in a community—a community as distinguished from a mere society, a mere functional organization. But this is a topic we shall come to later.

The relation of the self to society is more specifically the concern of *An American Tragedy*. For present purposes we can deal briefly with this complex masterpiece. Briefly, because it is an extension of Dreiser's earlier work into a new moment of American society. But, at least, we must look at its historical context.

The period after the Civil War was one of massive development. The "barbaric wealth" of the Barons and their hangers-on was a wealth from production, and the looting and stock-jobbery by which some wealth was notoriously accumulated was an extension of the more basic activity. For all its productivity, the United States was still, however, a debtor nation. It was not until 1918 that we became the great creditor nation, with fluidity and mobility increasing and the middle class on the rise, and with a new appetite for pleasure and for speculation in the market. There was, to sum up, a shift from the psychology of production to that of consumption. Modern advertising was born, to create a new dream, or, rather, a new phase of the American dream.

Clyde Griffiths is a son of old America and old values, with, significantly, street preachers for parents. But he, belonging to the new age, is the born consumer, with the passivity of the consumer, whose wishes are not only gratified, but created by the purveyor of goods. In his passivity he is the polar opposite of Cowperwood, the man of will. If Cowperwood's motto is "I please myself," that of Clyde would be, "I want you to please me." In contrast to Cowperwood's blazing, masterful gaze, we find Clyde's dark, yearning, "poetic" eyes. Before Cowperwood's eyes women shudder in fear and delight; before Clyde's they feel the impulse to help, to give. One is a ruthless taker, the other the cringing blackmailer. One uses women; the other all women use and command—except Roberta (and here we may recall that Dreiser confessed that he never made his way with women, that they always made their way with him). Significantly, Clyde "murders" Roberta only when she, the only woman whom he had ever sexually mastered, asserts her own will.

But does he "murder" her? He never knows. The event is ambiguous; and Clyde goes to the electric chair not knowing the nature of his act, nor knowing whether he has truly repented and now trusts God. His whole life has been a shadowy pursuit of fictive selves; a pursuit in which his very name had, for a while, been changed, to be reclaimed only when it was profitable to do so. The only constant content of his life has been yearning, and the belief in some magic, some genie to do his will: he has no self. Cowperwood is a "prince of dreams"; Clyde is the slave of dreams. Neither has a self in the final sense; but Cowperwood powerfully enacts his illusions, while Clyde suffers his. Both represent the poles of the "tragedy" of America, a land of fictive values seized, or yearned after, by fictive selves.

The literature of the period from 1920 to the Second World War is shot through by the same theme of self. We see how in *The Great Gatsby*, Fitzgerald sought a solution for the problem. Gatsby is the individual who, seeking by will to create an ideal self (as Clyde Griffiths, in his passivity, had yearned to do), ends in delusion and death; but the narrator Nick Carraway, who, like Gatsby, has entered into the world of fictive selves, goes back to the Midwest, where he—with Fitzgerald apparently—assumes that a moral identity and a right relation to society are still possible. Nick's dream is, however, as absurdly ironical as Huck Finn's dream of escaping to the "territory." We all know that the Middlewest was "civilized," too.

As for Faulkner, his myth of Yoknapatawpha County recurringly bears on the question of self. The most famous instances, among many, are Popeye in *Sanctuary* and Joe Christmas in *Light in August*, but we may well recall Mr. Compson, who, in *Absalom, Absalom*, sadly regarding the modern time, says to his son that there must once have been a world in which men "had the gift of living once or dying once instead of being diffused and scattered creatures drawn blindly from a grab bag and assembled"—a world in which men had been "integer for integer" more simple and complete. Faulkner, with his historical sense, dramatizes over and over again the necessary relation of self to the community, to a society which, more than the agglomeration of units, embodies a sense of vital relations among individuals, an ethos. To look further, he dramatizes man's relation to nature as an underpinning of man's relation to man. Therefore, the Faulknerian myth sees the modern world of finance capitalism and technology as converting the human being into the machine, a process best exemplified in Flem Snopes of *The Hamlet* and, again, Popeye.

If Faulkner could, in his Nobel speech, voice a faith in man's capacity to endure as man, Hemingway's indictment of modernity was more desperate, more radical, and more contemptuous. The image of the First World War is, for Hemingway, the image of a catastrophic bankruptcy of Western civilization and the collapse of all traditional values, and those who do not understand this fact are victims of the big words that have become obscene—"sacred" and "not in vain." When Frederick Henry, in *A Farewell to Arms*, leaps into the swollen Tagliamento River to escape the Italian battle police, he is baptized into a new condition, that of the total outsider, the man who has resigned from society: he must create, in a strange inversion of the story of Clyde Griffiths, the stoic ethic of the lonely hero.

The stance of the lonely hero hypnotized a generation; it brought into consciousness an attitude that was, in that age, and against the more obvious drive of the age, struggling for utterance. It flattered the maimed self, maimed because it had lost its moorings in society, with the dream of the superman, an updated variant of the dream that Dreiser had presented in Cowperwood. Hemingway's attitude, like Cowperwood's, seems to imply the creation of a self in a world of non-selves. The lonely hero seeks, indeed, to create a self, but if the valid self derives from a relation of the individual and society, then the absolute individualism of the lonely hero can only result in the creation of another fictive self. Hemingway is, as a matter of fact, a late and more hairy manifestation of Emerson's infantile vision of the infinitude and omnipotence of the self, of the "egotistical sublime"—which was the seamy side of his vision of the Jeffersonian men who would cast their vote "on their honor and on their conscience."

The list of writers after the First World War whose work embodies this basic issue would include almost every distinguished practitioner of the art. Obviously, Eliot and Pound are fundamentally important, and even the work of Frost, more indirectly but characteristically, involves the same issue. And when we come to the writers after the Second World War, we find the old theme compounded by the sense of the human being set against a maimed and even sadistic society, and find more and more a general spirit of protest, despair, aimlessness, violence, and amoral transactions at all levels.

Let us pause and look back. In one perspective our history seems little short of miraculous. Two hundred years ago a handful of men on the Atlantic seaboard, with a wild continent at the back, risked their necks and their sacred honor to found a new kind of nation, and thus unleashed an unprecedented energy that succeeded to a power and prosperity beyond their most fantastic dreams. Our "poetry" has celebrated this miraculous feat, and has been in itself—and let me emphasize this fact—a manifestation of that untamable energy that seized and occupied the continent.

Poetry, especially strong poetry, is not, however, more than superficially concerned with the celebration of objective victories. Greek tragedy, though it sprang from the energy and will that made Marathon and Samothrace possible, does not celebrate those victories, any more than *Hamlet* and *Lear* celebrate the defeat of the Spanish Armada. What poetry most significantly celebrates is the capacity of man to face the deep, dark inwardness of his nature and his fate. At the same time that we have seized and occupied our continent, our poets have explored the crisis of the American spirit grappling with its destiny. They have faced, sometimes unconsciously, the tragic ambiguity of the fact that the spirit of the nation we had promised to create has often been the victim of our astounding objective success, and that, in our success, we have put at pawn the very essence of the nation we had promised to create—that essence being the concept of the free man, the responsible self.

In other words, our poetry, in fulfilling its function of bringing us face to face with our nature and our fate, has told us, directly or indirectly, consciously or unconsciously, that we are driving toward the destruction of the very assumption on which our nation is presumably founded.

A bearer of ill tidings—and that is what our poetry, in one dimension, is—generally gets regarded as the guilty perpetrator of the disaster reported. Why, then, has our literature been taught in schools and colleges, been accepted, been applauded?

One simple answer is that a nation is supposed to have a literature and this is the only literature the United States has. But perhaps there is a complex of answers. There may be the answer that readers, readers in general, do not really read our literature for its deeper motives. It may be, too, that readers rarely confront our literature in a lump, its meaning as a whole. Moreover, we must recognize that very few people in our population read such books as I have been talking about. Certainly, at the upper end of the spectrum, men of practicality and power, the men who run society, do not generally read such books, but indulgently or contemptuously leave such toys to women, children, unformed college students, eggheads, longhairs, professors, and effete aesthetes.

There is, however, a more comforting reflection, a reflection made possible by our history. In America alienation has a somewhat different background from that found in Europe. The difference derives from two facts. First, insofar as the alienation in Europe was a reflex to the sudden rise of the industrial order, it was enormously exacerbated by the fact of the city as prison. The country man, lured to the city in the hope of liberation, might find a new and more dehumanizing prison, one in which none of the old comforting sanctions and values could apply; worse, the industrial city lay at the end of his road, the door was shut and the key was turned. In America, on the contrary, there was the West, infinite space and free land, and the dream of the possibilities this fact suggested colored actuality; the sense of entrapment came very late, with the industrial development after the Civil War, and with the massive immigration of that period.

Second, the concept of the significant self was here proclaimed in the Declaration of Independence, and embodied, a little later, in the very structure of the government which was to depend upon the vote of "single men spoken on their honor and their conscience." As for the social order, it was assumed to be open and fluid, a world in which the self could fulfill its possibilities.

Certainly, the real did not precisely conform to the ideal. Not many members of the "tumultuous populace of the large cities" of Washington's time managed to escape to an Eden over the mountains to be regenerated as Jeffersonian "selves"; even in the days of romantic democracy, neither government nor society fulfilled man's best hope; and after the Civil War, the industrial order, with the depersonalizing rigor that had traumatized the European soul, here began to flourish like the green bay tree. Granted all this, the general reaction, from the laborer on up to the philosopher or artist, was vastly different from that of, say, Gautier, who, by 1835, in the famous Preface to *Mademoiselle de Maupin*, had already proclaimed the bourgeoisie, with their passion for respectability, religion of utilitarianism, and philosophy of progress, to be dull as dishwater and as blunt-souled as brutes and the incorrigible enemy of art and the human spirit.

For Gautier, as for generations thereafter in Europe, there was only the irreconcilable quarrel between the artist and his world. But for the American writer, at least until the First World War, the quarrel was not, in general, with his world but with what had been made of his world. He was not alienated from the premise of his world, from what might be thought of as the spiritual reality of his world, and even when alienated from its actuality, he managed to cling to some hope that it might be redeemed. It should be remembered, too, that the United States, not the England of soap-boilers, was the bourgeois nation par excellence, in which, it might be said, the values of trade were transmogrified into the ideals of freedom; and it should be remembered, too, that European slogans have always sounded somewhat exotic here, and often irrelevant. It might be very romantic to shout, "Down with the bourgeosie!" But who, exactly, would the shouter be shouting about? He would be shouting about almost everybody he knew, including, certainly, the majority of the American "proletariat," with its passion for freezers, color TV, and eight-cylinder cars. And to compound confusion, he would be shouting about a segment of his own soul—and, in a long-range view, the very forces that, ironically, had given him the freedom to shout.

Long before the bad news from France and the

exquisites of *fin de siècle* London had reached us, we had patented our own version of alienation. Even after it became fashionable to speak of Rimbaud and Hart Crane in the same breath, we still had to admit that Eliot, and even Pound at his nuttiest, were concerned with the fate of society in a way that would have been totally incomprehensible to Gautier or Rimbaud. And in such a connection, who would ever think of Dreiser and Faulkner, or of Frost and Ransom? Even after our provincialism had been instructed, most of us clung to our home-grown variety of grief and a quaint, sneaking hope of reconciliation.

We may congratulate ourselves that this quaint hope survives. We may also congratulate ourselves that a certain number of our citizens do yearn for the enrichment and invigoration that poetry can afford even in the role of the bearer of *bad* tidings of great joy. In fact, the number of such citizens seems to be on the increase and some politicians are now inclined to make gestures toward the arts as well as toward motherhood, the Constitution, and American individualism.

Let us not, however, rest at ease in Zion. If we congratulate ourselves on the public recognition and support of the arts, we must remember that much private support is drying up, not merely from the unhealthy state of the economy, but as an indirect result of public policy. Furthermore, in the colleges and universities there is a reaction against the arts and humanities as impractical and "elitist." But let us turn to a straw in the more general wind, a passage from the White House tapes. Here the former President and his closest adviser are discussing how the President's daughters should spend their time before the opening of the Republican Convention of 1972:

> President: For example—now the worse thing (unintelligible) is to go to anything that has to do with the Arts.
>
> Haldeman: Ya, see that—it was (unintelligible) Julie giving [given?] that time in the Museum in Jacksonville.
>
> President: The Arts you know—they're Jews, they're left wing—in other words, stay away.

The passage is, clearly, the utterance of a paranoid, power-bit Philistine of no generosity of spirit, little imagination, and an education of the most limited technical sort—the blind striking out against whole dimensions of life which, because incomprehensible to him, seem to be, not only an affront to his vanity, but a sinister attack on his very being. But this passage may be more, a symptom of more general significance.

The forces that have made for the disintegration of the notion of the self, as reported in our literature, and dramatized therein, may be more powerful than ever. The inevitable result of this will be a literature—and an art in general—more critical, more alienated, than ever before, in the face of the dominant drive of the age. It may well be a poetry more acutely manifesting what Martin Buber has called "the most intimate of all

resistances—resistance to mass or collective loneliness."
Or at least a cry of pain and resentment in that situation.

What the powers of a new age will make of such sub-
versive voices remains to be seen.

Poetry and Selfhood

I AM GOING TO make some very sweeping generalizations here about everything from the history of science to the role of poetry, with flag stops at way stations such as human nature in general and the fate of the Western world. But I really don't want to make a noise like a doom-sayer, or even a pundit at large. As has been remarked, "it is now trivial to say that Western culture is undergoing a crisis, but it is not trivial to live it." So, in spite of my big generalizations and quotations from real pundits, what I want to do is to return us— myself most of all—to a scrutiny of our own experience of our own world. Each of us must live his own life, assess his own world, and discover his own satisfactions—and dissatisfactions. I suppose that this essay is fundamentally my own attempt to do just that. Perhaps I can find some echo in your experience.

41

In the preceding essay I looked back at our poetry as a record of the dwindling of our conception of the self. Then I was regarding poetry as "diagnostic," as a social document; I noted how it has analyzed and recorded a crucial ailment of our democracy: the progressive decay of the notion of the self. Now I am regarding poetry as "therapeutic"; I am trying to indicate how, in the end, in the face of the increasingly disintegrative forces in our society, poetry may affirm and reinforce the notion of the self. Though I hasten to say that the end of poetry is to be poetry, and that only insofar as it fulfills that end may it properly serve either diagnostic or therapeutic ends.

The subject of this book is "Democracy and Poetry," and I am going to take a long way around the barn to get back to it. I have to take a long way around, for we need a context if we are to understand the subject. That subject specifically is the meaning of poetry for democracy.

But first, how can democracy, as we conceive it, exist in a world of science, technology, and big organization? Without question, science, technology, and big organization have historically contributed to the development of democracy, and may again play such a role. But we are living in our moment, and in that moment we approach what Zbigniew Brzezinski calls the Technetronic Age. So, as he phrases it, the great question is, "Can the institutions of political democracy be adapted to the new conditions sufficiently quickly to meet the crises, yet without debasing their democratic character?" But behind this question looms a greater one, which he puts with perfect succinctness: "Can the individual and science [by which he presumably means the order that science has made possible] co-exist?"

As we approach the Technetronic Age, what some of us would regard as the less beneficent aspects of the modern order are emerging at an astronomical rate. In fact, such surly grumblings against the modern dispensation as were once characteristic of only a handful of disgruntled romantics has now become a deafening chorus of apocalyptic dismay, the chorus being largely composed of savants, philosophers, and hardheaded researchers of nothing less than world stature, but with no Sunday supplement or middlebrow magazine or college colloquium complete without a chic dash of doom. What these Jeremiahs and the Cassandras find fault with is nothing less than the proudest monument of our society: the overarching, interlocking, and mutually supportive structures of science, technology, and big organization.

Here we seem to be stuck with a paradox. On the one hand, we obviously cannot feed even the present population of the planet without those interlocking structures. But bread is not enough to keep man happy, as Rene Dubos, one among many of the new breed of grumblers, recently suggests in an essay entitled "Civilizing Technology." In fact, as Dubos declares, aggressive technology—technology that follows its internal logic without reference to the general context —may, ironically enough, deprive us, in the end, of bread itself.

Starvation is not the only threat advertised to us. Some people, oppressed by the great society-as-machine, predict, with perhaps a hint of self-congratulatory delight, the moment when all machines will go kaput. The world may end, not with a bang, but with a technological snafu, as D. H. Lawrence predicts in a poem, "The Triumph of the Machine":

So mechanical man in triumph seated upon the seat of his machine
will be driven mad from himself, and sightless, and on that day
the machines will turn to run into one another
traffic will tangle up in a long-drawn-out crash of collision . . .

Or there may be a bang, a more fundamental crack-up than Lawrence's relatively harmless little melodrama of the Jersey Turnpike. There is not only starvation to fear, the experts tell us: somebody may, really, drop the big bomb; the air may really get unbreatheable; industrial resources are finite and our demands increasing exponentially; the possibility of crossing the fatal threshold for heat emission seems to be sliding toward probability. We may, indeed, have become, as Erik Erikson describes us, "a species mortally dangerous to it-self." Or we may be approaching an age of bloody troubles to be followed, perhaps, by a neo-primitivism in which time will die into the mere succession of the seasons and history will die into ritual.

Out of an age of troubles, however, some regime other than that of neo-primitivism to guarantee survival might emerge—some regime even less to our taste. Further-more, since for most of us any authentic civilization must be "democratic," it is ominous to reflect that democracy cannot exist in a society that is merely a mechanism for satisfying man's physical needs and keeping order. A mechanistic society cannot, on the one hand, accommodate what John Stuart Mill long ago took, and what many of us are still old-fashioned enough to take, to be the basis of liberty: a variety of character and the chance for human nature to expand in different and even contradictory directions. Nor, on the other hand, can such a society foster a com-munity of individual selves bound together by common feelings, ideals, and conceptions of responsibility. And to achieve this, in the face of our exfoliating problems of mere survival, would entail, as a multitude of prophets have proclaimed, the creation of a new body of attitudes and values, a new assessment of our expand-ing technological capacities in relation to the context of nature and our basic human needs.

And in this connection here is the Port Huron State-ment of Students for a Democratic Society, as issued in

1962, long before that organization had found ways to make itself newsworthy:

> We regard *men* as infinitely precious and possessed of unfulfilled capacities for reason, freedom, and love . . . We oppose the depersonalization that reduces human beings to the status of things. If anything, the brutalities of the twentieth century teach that means and ends are intimately related.

Even if the brutalities of the twentieth century were *not* enough, in the light of the subsequent record, to teach the SDS that means and ends are intimately related, who could take exception to their Statement as the description of a desirable "consciousness"?

I do not know how such a consciousness is to be achieved, but I do know some of the things that will not achieve it: wearing bell-bottom trousers, navel-watching, hammering copper wire, burning the Beinecke Library of Yale or any other, enforcing censorship by intimidation or violence, substituting rock for Beethoven, or LSD for the painter's palette, or imagining a vain thing, one vain thing being that *authenticity* is a magic word to summon spirits from the vasty deep. The "authentic" doing of one's "thing" may involve anything from cretinism to crime—neither of which provides an exclusively reliable index to the existence of an immortal soul. "Authenticity" is merely one of the two poles of action, and the other pole is a sense of objective standards, just as the individual is one pole of the existence of the self, and the other, society, or more specifically, community. To put the matter into literary terms, the only "authentic" utterance is the scream of agony or the moan of bliss: solipsism.

But let us turn to the nature of the world we now inhabit. It is the world of science, technology, big organization—and of course the business culture. As for science, the end of man is to know. Man has more curiosity than the cat that, in the adage, got killed by it, but so far curiosity has not killed man—even though for more than a century thinkers of great eminence, including such disparate characters as Henry Adams, Jacob Burckhardt, Sigmund Freud, Aldous Huxley, and Lewis Mumford have expressed the fear that the kind of knowledge brought forth by scientific curiosity might wind up doing just that. Be that as it may, those thinkers, and a multitude of others, have raised another question: Even though overwhelmed by the grandeur and apparent inevitability of the scientific project, does man, nevertheless, still yearn for other kinds of knowledge? Not in place of, but in addition to, scientific knowledge, in order to make a world more humanly habitable? Even in the Age of Enlightenment, the lonely and then little-known humanist Giambattista Vico could rebel against the universalizing and abstracting norms of Cartesian thought and assert the need for the study of individuating forms; where Descartes had regarded poetry and history as little more than "chaotic visions," Vico proclaimed poetry as a "primary activity of mind," an activity without which language, philosophy, and civilization itself could not have developed, not a mere device for the popular dissemination of truth nor a diversion of the mind; and to the mathematical knowledge fundamental for Descartes, he added a knowledge based on the empathic imagination, which could, for instance, penetrate into what he calls the "poetic wisdom" of earlier mankind, the intuitive comprehension of history based on the fact of a common humanity. And a century later, even in the age when the new positivism was seizing the minds of men, Søren Kierkegaard affirmed that abstract thought cannot grasp the meaning of existence and that feeling—passion, as he termed it —provides the knowledge that is the key of existence and action. More recently we find Bertrand Russell's distinction between "power knowledge," the knowledge given by science, and "love knowledge," the knowledge that comes from the intuitive and imagination grasp of nature and man. But can the kind of knowledge that Vico, the Romantic poets, Kierkegaard, and Russell speak of survive into our world? Or will the continual presence of abstraction in man's thought dry up, as Santayana once suggested, the old springs of poetry? If "love knowledge" and intuition and imagination are on the wane, is it because man's "calculation," to use Shelley's terms in *The Defence of Poetry*, has outrun his "conception"?

Even the most scientifically uninstructed among us—

and I refer to myself—can read the account. When Galileo set his eye to the telescope, he stepped off the terrestial globe into uncharted space. He had leaped to a point from which to look back on the little globe—an "Archimedean point," it has been called. Long before, the Syracusan sage had boasted that if he had a lever long enough and a place whereon to rest it he could move the world, and now Galileo had found such a point whereon he might rest the lever of his question about the structure of the universe. That point was to become, we are told, the fulcrum on which rests the lever of all modern science, which does move the world.

Galileo's contemporary, Descartes, also stepped off the terrestial globe, though in quite a different fashion. Doubt, radical doubt, was his Archimedean point; and when he proclaimed doubt of both the evidence of the senses and the testimony of reason, he withdrew from contact with the world as men had been experiencing it. It was to be harder and harder for men ever again to experience that old, full-bodied world. As Yeats, in a half-echo of Blake's poem "The Atoms of Democritus," put it in *Explorations*, "Descartes, Locke, and Newton took away the world and gave us its excrement instead" —the excrement being the quantified world, the shadow-world, of science.

Man could not, in fact, be sure that the quantified world actually referred to any real, objective world whatsoever. The only certainty promised by Descartes inhered in his famous utterance, "Cogito ergo sum," the certainty available to man in his scrutiny of his own intellectual processes. Men might know this much, anyway, and in such a lonely, locked-in condition, some men might even exult, as Yeats does, paradoxically enough, in the second of "Two Songs from a Play," when he celebrates the imaginative power that redeems man's isolation:

> Whatever flames upon the night
> By man's own resinous heart is fed.

There are, however, many who cannot exult, and therefore suffer from metaphysical claustrophobia. Not only may there be no objective world beyond the locked lid of the box, but the locked-in man may himself be only a dream, to boot. Dream or not, he suffers uncertainty, an uncertainty that Descartes could alleviate by the appeal to God's goodness. But even if there is a God, His goodness is not always apparent, and so another nightmare, as Hannah Arendt refers to it, comes—that of the *Dieu trompeur*. The Jokester God has always existed, as poor Job well knew, or as Calvin and Hobbes advertised, but the post-Cartesian form is special, a God who creates man with a passion for truth and then denies him any access to it, even to a truth about his own existence.*

---

*To revert to our first essay, it is Mark Twain who, in his later years, was most obviously tortured by his special versions of the post-Cartesian

In the Cartesian epoch, however, before the night-mares began to afflict him, man conceived of the universe as a watch that had long ago been wound up—a machine which, though the best of all possible machines, was a machine. As for man himself, he was to become a machine, too. So much for the record.

There is, however, a sequel. With the emergence of quantum physics, the big machine model of the universe, we are told, blew up and the old doctrine of determinism was called into question. Mathematical equations took the place of the machine, and even if the equations did enunciate world-shaking truths, the truths weren't the old rock-ribbed variety associated with the machine, and the very ghostliness of the equations seems to have led scientists themselves, some of them anyway, to say, with Alfred North Whitehead, that, "if civilization is to survive, the expansion of understanding is a prime necessity," and, with Edmund W. Sinnott, that "teleology, far from being unscientific, is implicit in the very nature of organism." Some even began to refer to artists as brother symbolists with merely a different kind of net for snaring "reality."

nightmare; that of loss of the objective world and of the self (which for him, with his pathology of guilt was paradoxically a blessing), and that of the *Dieu trompeur*. The presence of that *Dieu trompeur* is sometimes merely felt, as in the end of *A Connecticut Yankee*, but later he appears in person, as in *The Mysterious Stranger*. Hemingway, too, suffered from the post-Cartesian nightmare, in a somewhat more modern version than Twain's, for instance, in "A Clean Well-Lighted Place," where the Lord's Prayer is prayed to *nada*, in *nada*, and for *nada*.

Here I am tempted to construct a little fairy tale: Once upon a time, there was a bumbling and kind-hearted old father named Science, and he had a smart, brawny son who found the father's way of life dull, and so set forth to make his fortune. Not far on his journey he met a beautiful golden-haired lady with a bewitching smile. Her name was Money. Now Money had a bad reputation in certain quarters, especially among old, stuffy folk, and it was even rumored that she had borne several bastards. But bastards or no, she had never lost her girlishly lissome figure, delicious complexion, promising smile, and eye for brawny young fellows. Of course this young fellow, having been raised in so retired a way, knew nothing of the gossip about the lady. So they got married and lived happily ever after—at least, until right now—for he was blind to her little private diversions and was wrapped up in a beautiful, thriving little son who grew as fast as a beanstalk and whose name was Business Culture. I forgot to tell you that the brawny young fellow who married the durable lady was named Technology.

Well, to get serious again, the kind of technology we have does not seem to derive from the more open-ended and inclusive views which rumor instructs me are to be found in current scientific thought. Our reigning variety of technology seems to have branched off from science in the age of machine as model, and that gave the image that has been carried into the heart of man. It is the image that still affects his relation to nature, to other men, and to himself.

As for nature, "The Heavens declare the glory of God," according to the Psalmist, and even a latter-day philosopher, Santayana, remarks that nature, though offering "no transcendental logic" and "no sign of any deliberate morality seated in the world," may stir the "super-human possibilities of your own spirit." But nature can also be regarded as a machine, and as such, can be manipulated, sometimes enslaved. As for men, they can also be regarded as machines—not as souls or selves—and can be manipulated. But by whom? By other machines, of course, for the manipulator is only a man, too.

Technology not only carried the image of machine as model into man's consciousness; it provided him with quite literal machines, which, in turn, altered his consciousness. For one thing, it profoundly altered his sense of time. Before the Industrial Revolution, no individual man ever experienced change. Great changes did occur, but the ordinary man did not know them. What he knew was vicissitude, wars, famines, floods, the fall of dynasties, but the basic pattern of existence, insofar as it was visible in any one man's life, did not change. Suddenly, change was visible and tangible, and that change was occurring in a constantly accelerating system which undercut inherited sanctions and values in a progressive disorientation of the sense of time and a rupture of all aspects of human continuity. With this disorientation the self, in a strange new loneliness, fell sick. Man began to feel even more acutely cut off from nature, and in addition cut off from society, from a sense of significance in his work, from, in the end, any sense of significance in his own existence. Alienation, in various forms, appeared.

In America, however, in the beginning anyway, man did not feel a disorientation in his sense of time, but a liberation from time. Even if Jefferson had declared that the study of history should be basic for the education of the free citizen, space replaced time as the prime category for that citizen; and man, moving ever westward, was redeemed from the past, was washed in the Blood of a new kind of Lamb. This sense of liberation was, of course, compounded by the American's confidence in his know-how, and Henry Ford would eventually sum matters up: "History is bunk."

So Americans, long back, developed their secular millennialism, which, developing out of the old theology, gave our citizens the conviction of being on the Great Gravy Train, with a first-class ticket. It is easy to see how we arrived at this notion. Our forefathers did have wonderful confidence and energy; as Thomas Jefferson, in a letter to his daughter Martha, remarked, Americans felt that any difficulty could be surmounted by "resolution" and "contrivance"—and this remained as true of the last man off the boat at Ellis Island as of the first settler at Jamestown. But the success that rewarded our resolution and contrivance led us, bit by bit, to believe that solutions would be almost automatic: pass a law, take a poll, draw up a budget, make a body count, hire an expert or PR man, believe only optimistic reports. There is no use in rehearsing the long list of consequences of this attitude, but we may name a few: sick cities, blighted landscapes, an irrational economy, a farcical educational system, and a galloping inflation, not to mention the fact that, after spending astronomical sums, committing massive technical equipment, and suffering heavy casualties, we got the be-Jesus kicked out of us in the jungles of Asia. But we are still the City set on a Hill—or think we are—and the Chosen People with a hotline to the Most High.

Perhaps we are, indeed, the Chosen People—and I should like to think that we are. But it is hard work to stay "chosen," and it is harder to scrutinize our situation and ourselves when our chosenness seems to wear a little thin. And hard to realize that there may be no more automatic solutions, even for us. This is not pessimism. It is, rather, optimism—in the sense that it implies confidence in our will to be, not victims, but makers, of our history. But that optimism implies, too, that we must try to look at ourselves, to recognize that we are not free from the hazards of selfhood, nor of time.

If history, as J. H. Plumb grimly speculated in *The Death of the Past*, cannot survive as a study, then its role "as the interpreter of men's destiny will be taken by the social sciences." Which is to say that the ideal of understanding men and telling their story, noble or vicious, will be replaced by the study of statistics or nonideographic units of an infinite series, and computers will dictate how such units, which do breathe and move, can best be manipulated for their own good. We may not be there yet, but we are on the way, for the contempt of the past inevitably means that the self we have is more and more a fictive self, the self of a non-ideographic unit, for any true self is not only the result of a vital relation with a community but is also a development in time, and if there is no past there can be no self.

Furthermore, a society with no sense of the past, with no sense of the human role as significant not merely in experiencing history but in creating it can have no sense of destiny. And what kind of society is it that has no sense of destiny and no sense of self? That has no need or will to measure itself by the record of human achievement and the range of the human endowment? And here we may pause to ask what our society measures itself by. Is it only by the ability to gratify immediate appetites, capacity for consumption, and the GNP?

The effect of the abolition of the past on the conception of the self is by a negative, by denying the individual the chance to see himself in the perspective of human nature and human accomplishment. But our world also exercises positive effects of the first magnitude on the individual's sense of self. Before entering upon this topic we must, however, grant that in all times and places man has necessarily lived a large part of his life in what Martin Buber calls the realm of *It*—the realm of economics, politics, science, military activity, labor, and so on—as contrasted with the realm of *Thou*, in which massive relations of recognition and reverence may prevail. In our age, however, the realm of *It* has become progressively enlarged, and indeed must be enlarged if we are to enjoy certain manifest benefits. The doctor cannot cure us unless he "it-ifies" us: he must ignore the immortal soul and take a blood test. And if our soul is sick, the psychiatrist must also do some "it-ifying." So in our contact with technology and big organization we are most often, by necessity and definition, in the realm of *It*. We are numbers on cards, and in the schoolroom as on the production line identity bleeds away; and, in all big organizations, the individual is necessarily regarded as an expendable, because replaceable, part.

Jacques Ellul, the French sociologist, argues furthermore that the important fact is not the individual's relation to any one field of technology, but what he calls the "phenomenon of technical convergence." This is the convergence on man of a plurality of systems or complexes of techniques. Even though "each individual technician can assert in good faith that his technique leaves intact the integrity of its object," the problem concerns not his technique, but the convergence on the individual of all techniques as a "completely spontaneous phenomenon, representing a normal stage in the evolution of technique." It concerns, in the end, how man "feels" about himself, and socially how he behaves.

Ellul is referring to what we may call a centripetal effect, that of many forces bearing in from the periphery toward the individual, each with its implied message that the individual is not really a "self" but a machine. But there are, in addition, centrifugal forces from the center, which is the individual. In the modern world the individual emerges from his basic anonymity, which is the very matrix of life in that world, to perform briefly some business or social role, which varies from occasion to occasion. And here a paradox seems to be built into our world. On the one hand, we know that our ability to act effectively is intimately related to, or is even an index of, the sense of the self. On the other hand, effective action in our world seems to imply more and more the denial of any central self. So, somehow bolstered and justified by vulgarizations of various notions of relativity, from physics through anthropology to philosophical pragmatism, the ordinary, decent, intelligent citizen, functioning in the morally neutral world of technologies, easily begins to assume that the only self worth having is one to be defined primarily by its capacity to deny its "self." Fluidity of selves replaces the integrity of self as the source of effectiveness, and identity is conceived in terms of mere

action, with action determined completely by the fluc-
tuating contingencies of the environment.

Be that as it may, the sense of a continuing self—of
a ringmaster self, a self that exists between the assumed
roles—tends to be lost in the multiplicity of roles; worse,
the assumed roles are not merely multiple, they are often
contradictory, each demanding a spurious self that is the
price paid for success. Furthermore, for particularly
crucial transactions, we have public relations experts
who manufacture the appropriate self—a purely dra-
maturgical self, an *ad hoc* persona, which one buys with
the expectation of selling it at a profit to the public.

As for the public, the PR man, like the advertising
expert and others who deal with people in the lump,
including a number of would-be statesmen and redeem-
ers-at-large, conceive of that body as composed of
non-ideographic units which are to be regarded not as
selves but as, ultimately, gadgets of electrochemical
circuitry operated by a push-button system of remote
control. In fact, in dealing with the public in a purely
technological society, the very notion of self is bypassed
by various appeals to an undifferentiated unconscious,
such appeals often having little or no relation to the
vendible object or idea; in this connection history gives
us to contemplate the fact that the psychologist J. B.
Watson, the founder of American behaviorism, wound
up in the advertising business. So history may become
parable.

But to continue our comment on that business itself,

the very system that denies the existence of a self may, as a final irony, exploit the individual's hunger to achieve a self. Even a brand of milk has the slogan, "Drink Milk for a New You." Correspondence courses in piano playing (with a picture of "you" sitting down at the piano), sex manuals, face lotions, moonlit nights on the Caribbean as pictured in cruise ads, quickie psychology books—all offer a "New You." In the world of shadowy "you's" it is not significant that the "New You" advertised be a "central you"; it may just as well be a longed-for "role you"—the only kind of "you," in fact, that many of us can now conceive of. For, as Daniel Boorstin has so wittingly documented, the image is all.

As for the image being ultimately merchandised to you, it is of "You-as-Consumer." The fundamental role of the citizen is no longer that of producer but of consumer, and for patriotic virtue, "brand loyalty" ranks next to the Oath of Allegiance and the singing commercial next to "The Star-Spangled Banner."

So we have Auden's little poem entitled:

> The Unknown Citizen
> (to JS/ 07/ M378)
> This Marble Monument
> Is Erected by the State

It begins:

He was found by the Bureau of Statistics to be
One against whom there was no official complaint,
And all the reports of his conduct agree
That, in the modern sense of an old-fashioned word,
    he was a saint.

The Unknown Citizen is the Saint of Consumption, the Unknown Soldier of the Undifferentiated Unconscious of the Consuming Public.

In 1846, in "The Present Age," Søren Kierkegaard remarked on the nature of the public and its relation to the self. The public, he said, is a "body that can never be reviewed; it cannot even be represented, because it is an abstraction." When the age is, as he declared his age to be, "passionless and destroys everything concrete, the public becomes everything and is supposed to include everything."

He went on to examine the nature of that abstraction which the "public" is: "A generation, a people, an assembly of the people, a meeting, or a man are responsible for what they are and can be made ashamed if they are inconstant and unfaithful; but a public remains a public." When the individual "really is what he is, he does not form part of the public. Made up of such individuals, of individuals at the moments when they are nothing, a public is a kind of gigantic something, an abstract and deserted void which is everything but nothing."

Now Kierkegaard was a Christian and believed in the immortal soul. Even so, he held that the individual needed social support for the self: "The real moment in time and the real situation of being simultaneous with real people each of whom is something—that is what helps to sustain the individual." And that was what he found lacking in *his* "modern world." What of *our* "modern world," with not even an immortal soul, and with a public that resembles the physicist's conception of the "black hole"—a devouring negativity. Where do we find the "real people each of whom is something" and who may, therefore, sustain us?

Kierkegaard is not saying, it should be emphasized, that there was a time before his "modern" age when men were better, more virtuous, more noble. "Betterness" is not the point. "Realness" is the point. To illustrate what is at stake here, let us take a famous street scene in a poem by Jonathan Swift, "A City Shower." Here London types of the eighteenth century are pictured as caught in the bad weather—the dandy, the blade, the seamstress, the needy poet, and the young lawyer; and the poem ends with swollen gutters and flooded streets, the whole city awash in secret filth now flushed to light:

Sweepings from butcher's stalls, dung, guts, and blood,
Drowned puppies, stinking sprats, all drenched in mud,
Dead cats and turnip-tops come tumbling down the
    flood.

Here, with the last word, the literal scene becomes an image of the Deluge, with the literal offal and waste an image of man's moral filth.

My point is that Swift's London is inhabited by creatures who, being human, being "real," are subject to moral judgment. But when we come into the nineteenth century we find, for instance, Baudelaire's picture of the streets of Paris, in which the nightmare is not of evil but of unreality, most notably in "Les Sept Vieillards," which begins:

> Fourmillante cité, cité plein de reves,
> Où le spectre en plein jour raccroche le passant!

In the ant-swarm of the city, it is the specter, not a human being, that, in broad daylight, keeps grabbing the passerby. And in our century it is not in the Paris street but over London Bridge (or in the New York subway) that the crowd prompts the poet to exclaim, in an echo of the appalled utterance of Dante in Hell, "I had not thought death had undone so many."* Meanwhile, long

---

*On this matter of the view of the specters, Raymond Williams, like many other men of good will, would argue, as he does in *Culture and Society* (New York, 1958, pp. 297-332), that the sense of the unreality in the "mass," in "others"—even the casual use of the word *mass* as in "mass democracy" or "mass media"—springs from an unconscious elitism or class pride, or simply from a failure in humane imagination. Let us grant that this stricture has some justice. But we must also remember that in this modern situation the individual, the *passant* who is grabbed by the specter, does not congratulate himself on his own superior reality. The sense of the unreality of others, of

before Eliot et al., the Romantic poets had discovered
their painfully ambiguous relation to society, and even
Tennyson, in the swinging meters of "Locksley Hall," had
meditated on man's new plight, declaring:

the other *passant* who is the specter, is only the obverse of a psychological
coin, the reverse of which is the individual's sense of his own unreality—of
alienation, anomie, displacement, devaluation. That is, in Baudelaire's poem,
the poet who sees the other *passant* as a *spectre* will declare himself, at the end,

Blessé par le mystère et par l'absurdité.

The mystery and the absurdity have so wounded the poet—or Everyman
—that, now sick, chilled to the bone, and disoriented, he locks his door
against the street. The man who sees the "de-selfed men" recognizes them
because he himself is "de-selfed." Baudelaire is explicit on this point. "We,"
he says, in his posthumous pieces under the title *Fusees*, "shall perish from
that by which we have expected to live." *All* men, that is, are fellow-
sufferers from "le progrès," which, he says, will "Americanize" the world
and kill "la partie spirituelle." Whatever debates there are among philoso-
phers and psychologists about the genesis of the self, we know that it is
inextricably related to the world around and to other selves.

Eliot presents, of course, other examples of specters, of the de-selfed, the
maimed, and the alienated. In Part III of "preludes," the woman—the "you"
—who wakes at dawn and lies on her back to watch the "thousand sordid
images" that "flicker up against the ceiling" has no self beyond that
"constituted" by the images. "The Love Song of J. Alfred Prufrock" can be
regarded as the anatomizing of various types of alienation. There is, first,
the alienation of the elite, social and artistic, that constitute the world of
Prufrock. Second, there is the alienation of the true artist from the elite
(what would Michelangelo do here?). Third, there is the alienation of
Prufrock himself from his elite world, insofar as he might try to be serious,
to take, we may say, his role as Lazarus. Fourth, there is Prufrock's aliena-
tion (and that of his world) from physical reality (from the sea-floor of the
"ragged claws"), and, as a corollary, the alienation from the world of
common life. But that world of common life may also offer its own type of
alienation, as is testified by the "lonely men in shirt sleeves leaning out
of windows." Prufrock's "nostalgic poetry of the *faubourg*," which Wallace
Fowlie (*Rimbaud*, Chicago, 1965, p. 205) says was invented by Rimbaud and
Laforgue, involves a more complex alienation than that of the inventors.

And the individual withers, and the world is more and
more.

Dostoevski, in *The House of the Dead*, that narrative of
prison life in Siberia, had presented a full-blown picture
of the modern world of alienation, men from all dif-
ferent regions and races of Russia now thrown to-
gether but each isolated and groping. Marx refers to his
world as one in which "truth is without passion, and
passion is without truth." And Baudelaire, in *Mon coeur
mis a nu*, had said of the same world, that decent men were
cowardly or soft, and "only the brigands" had "con-
victions," anticipating Yeats's description, in "The Sec-
ond Coming," of a world in which the best lack all
conviction and the worst are full of passionate intensity.

According to all these diagnoses, the individual fades
into abstraction, into various successive, shadowy roles,
with the highest abstraction, as Jung describes the
matter, being the "idea of the State as the principle of
political reality." Thus, the moral responsibility of the
individual, a mark of his selfhood, is "inevitably replaced
by the policy of the State," and the "moral and mental
differentiations of the individual" replaced by "public
welfare and the raising of the living standard." The
self is absorbed, ultimately, into *le raison d'état*—a situation
which we have seen totally realized in some regimes of
our century, and of which we have lately been able to
detect a few symptoms in our own land.

So it would seem that our technical mastery has not

brought us a longed-for freedom. As Engels long ago summarized it, if man "has subdued the forces of nature, the latter avenge themselves upon him by subjecting him, in so far as he employs them, to a veritable despotism independent of *all social organization*." But Engels was not referring to the most crucial assault, that on the very basis of freedom: the conception of the self. If this is the great source of our spiritual malaise, what can be done?

Change man, certain technologists answer. Man may be conditioned to become a really frictionless unit in the imminent technetronic apparatus—the "brave, new world," as Aldous Huxley famously called it. Some people grudgingly accept such a prospect as the only means of survival on an overpopulated planet, and others welcome it as a blessed relief from the burdens of selfhood or as a mystic marriage with the infinite. For instance, some of my operatives in graduate schools report that a certain type of young Ph.D. candidate in political science shivers with manic glee at the prospect of being a nameless cog in such a glittering and flawless new construct. This type, I am also told, resembles nothing so much as the young men of the Victorian age, who, falling in love with the doctrine of Progress, joyfully intoned the heady lines of Tennyson's "Locksley Hall":

Not in vain the distance beacons. Forward, forward let
  us range.
Let the great world spin forever down the ringing
  grooves of change.

So we would find here a stage beyond the absorption of
the self into *le raison d'etât*—the absorption into *le raison
de l'Administration Centrale des Ordinateurs*, which would be
housed, no doubt, in a massive palace of stainless steel
and glittering glass.

If some grumpy old codger objects that in this cyber-
netic heaven, man will lose his moral identity, the
technician's reply is that man is conditioned anyway, and
so why not do the job properly to give perfect function.
We might even improve on the technician's reply and
suggest that if the technicians are as expert as they
think they are—and they may well be—they can so
perfectly condition man that he will *feel* himself to exert
the moral will, and *feel* the joy of effort in growth and
fulfillment—all this to a degree far beyond what is
possible in our hit-or-miss and failure-fraught old-
fashioned life. Thus, the conditioners would really
bring us full circle, and the post-Cartesian nightmare
of the unreality of the world and the self would be
converted, by a benign dramaturgy, into a continuous
daydream so expertly staged, lighted, and directed that
it becomes "real" and thus the non-self would turn out
to be the best self after all.

But perhaps this is but the supreme secularization of our old millennial dream.

Earlier I have insisted that the long drift of our American democracy has been *toward* the abolition of the self. I have also insisted on the probability that as this process accelerates, our "poetry" will be found more subversive of the status quo, more alienated from the "specious good" which modern technological society has delivered to man as the ultimate good. (I here borrow a phrase from Lionel Trilling, which he in turn acknowledges he found in Wallace Fowlie's book on Rimbaud.) One effect of this situation will be to drive the solid citizen further from all art, except what is ritual or entertainment, and another will be to deepen among practical men a suspicion of anything that does not promise concrete profit to the constituency, and another will be to dry up funds, private and public, as investment or as grants, for what is not more or less immediately commercial—that is, for art that is not, in the most obvious sense, "democratic" —which will mean vendible.

But what—and this is the question to which I have been driving all along—is *really* democratic? I propose the simple answer that whatever works to make democracy possible is "really" democratic. And it would seem clear that "poetry" is an essential one of the "whatevers." For poetry—the work of the "makers"—is a dynamic affirmation of, as well as the image of, the concept of the self.

"*Resistance to the organized mass,*" Jung asserts (italics his), "*can be effective only by the man who is as well organized in his individuality as the mass itself.*" And we may argue that the "made thing"—the poem, the work of art—stands as a "model" of the organized self. This is not to claim that the poet who constructs this model is necessarily such an organized self. As a matter of fact, an appalling number of poets have been notoriously disorganized; though some, among them some of the greatest, have apparently been extremely well organized and died with sincere mourners at the bedside and, even, money in the bank.

It may perhaps be said, however, that even if the poet is disorganized, out of disorder may emerge the organized object: the image of the "ideal self," the "regenerate self," as it were, of the disorganized man. The poet's own disorganization may seem, on the record, merely personal, but more often than not the poem he produces brings to focus and embodies issues and conflicts that permeate the circumambient society, with the result that the poem itself evokes mysterious echoes in the selves of those who are drawn to it, thus providing a dialectic in the social process. The "made thing" becomes, then, a vital emblem of the struggle toward the achieving of the self, and that mark of struggle, the human signature, is what gives the aesthetic organization its numinousness. It is what makes us feel that the "made thing" nods mysteriously at us, at the deepest personal inward self.

The "made things" may belong to any of various orders of art. But let us think specifically of literature. Here the function of the work may be considered in two ways: what is said and the way of the saying; content and form. As for the content of a poem, fiction, or drama, there is always, presented or implied, an action, a conflict. Often there is a specified character on whom a work hinges and whose fate we follow, a Raskolnikov or a Hamlet, and in such cases the issue we have been talking about is clear.

But in all such cases, only insofar as the work establishes and expresses a self can it engage us. We observe this "model" of self in its adventures of selfhood. The torn self may find redemption, as with Oedipus or Lear. Or it may, as with Clyde Griffiths in *An American Tragedy*, affirm the nature and meaning of a self only in the painful story of the individual who lacks the very notion of selfhood. Or it may, as with Heller's *Catch 22* or Pyncheon's *V*, exhibit a maniacal world in which automatism has replaced self.

Thus far we have been speaking of works which present an objective and identifiable character. But even a lyric poem posits some self that is moved to utterance. The posited self of a lyric may be taken as purely fictional or as a shadowy persona of a literal self, the author. And this fact leads to the most subtle, complex, and profound relationship in literature. Even the work with the most objective and clearly delineated characters presented in action, such as Raskolnikov or Hamlet, exists only because there is a story behind the objective story; there is the story of the relation of the self of the author to the work created. It is not only the objective characters that serve as "models" of selfhood; the work itself represents the author's adventure in selfhood. As both Rilke and Yeats have put it, the making of a work represents a plunge into the "abyss of the self."* And once the work is made, the reader, insofar as he gives himself to it, takes such a plunge, too—the plunge to explore the possibilities of his own "abyss." In the complexity of this whole situation we find, then, echo upon echo, or mirror facing mirror. But in the end, as Henri Bergson once said, the work returns us—the readers, the spectators—"into our own presence." It wakes us up to our own life.

As for form, we may begin with the general notion that man is the form-making animal. Other animals, indeed,

*Art, as Rilke conceives it, "is a movement contrary to nature." He continues: "No doubt God never foresaw that any one of us would turn inward upon himself in this way, which can only be permitted to the Saint because he seeks to beseige his God by attacking him from this unexpected and badly defended quarter. But for the rest of us, whom do we approach when we turn our back on events, on our future even, in order to throw ourselves into the abyss of our being, which would engulf us were it not for the sort of truthfulness that we bring to it, and which seems stronger even than the gravitation of our nature . . . it is we who are the real awakeners of our [inward] monsters, to which we are not hostile enough to become their conquerors . . . it is they, the monsters, that hold the surplus strength which is indispensable to those that must surpass themselves." (Letters to Merline, tr. Violet M. MacDonald, London, 1951, p. 48.)

The statement from Yeats runs: "Why should we honor those that die upon the field of battle, a man may show as reckless a courage in entering into the abyss of himself." (Quoted in Richard Ellmann, Yeats: The Man and the Masks, New York, 1948, p. 6.)

71

make forms and some seem to be thrusting toward the human kind of form-making; but man remains the form-making animal par excellence. By making forms he understands the world, grasps the world, imposes himself upon the world. But the "made thing" that the poet produces represents a different kind of form from all the others we know. Its characteristic quality springs from the special fullness of the relation of a self to the world. The form of a work represents, not only a manipulation of the world, but an adventure in selfhood. It embodies the experience of a self vis-à-vis the world, not merely as a subject matter, but as translated into the experience of form. The form represents uniqueness made available to others, but the strange fact is that the uniqueness is not to be exhausted: the "made thing" does not become a Euclidian theorem any more than love is exhausted by the sexual act. The "made thing," the "formed thing," stands as a perennial possibility of experience, available whenever we turn to it; and insofar as we again, in any deep sense, open the imagination to it, it provides the freshness and immediacy of experience that returns us to ourselves and, as Nietzsche puts it, provides us with that "vision," that "enchantment," which is, for man, the "completion of his state" and an affirmation of his sense of life.

From such a general notion, let us turn to at least one special aspect of the work as a form, an aspect that has to do with the context of our present world. The self has been maimed in our society because, for one reason, we lose contact with the world's body, lose any holistic sense of our relation to the world, not merely in that there is a split between emotion and idea but also because perception and sensation are at a discount—except when set off from the fullness of life and marketed as sensationalism. If Keats exclaimed, "Oh, for a life of sensations rather than thoughts!" he was not denying the wholeness of the vital emblems which his poems are. He cried out for sensation only because he felt that "sensation" was what his "modern world" denied him.

So Wordsworth had demanded that he might "enjoy" what others only "understand." And when Prufrock, a century later, declares that he should have been a "pair of ragged claws" scuttling across the sea floor, we have again the cry of a man stifled by a world of abstraction. So in D. H. Lawrence's poem "Cry of the Masses":

> Give us back, Oh give us back
> Our bodies before we die!

So with Imagism, Pound's poetry, Hemingway's declarative sentence, William Carlos William's slogan "No ideas but in things,"Paul Klee's intention not to reflect but to make visible the world, and Conrad's phrasing of his deepest hope as an artist, "Before all, to make you see!"

No one has cried out, "Before all, to make you hear!" But that effort has proceeded, it goes without saying, with every new musical composition; and it has proceeded, too, with every new style of prose or verse, with all the struggle to discover new principles of form that have characterized our century. And here, to take only one aspect of form, I must insist that even in literature rhythm—not mere meter, but all the pulse of movement, density, and shadings of intensity of feeling—is the most intimate and compelling factor revealing to us the nature of the "made thing." Furthermore, by provoking a massive re-enactment, both muscular and nervous, of the quality of language (or other medium, if we speak of another art), it binds our very physiological being to it in the context of the rhythms of the universe. This same principle holds true of other archetectonic sorts of rhythm, as in a static structure, a bridge or building— or in a play or poem in which we can envisage a structure out of time as well as experience the sequential rhythms in time. And when we experience the contrast and interplay of rhythms of time and movement with those of non-time and stasis—that is, when we grasp a work in relation to the two orders of rhythm and both in terms of felt meaning—what a glorious *klang* of being awakens to unify mind and body, to repair, if even for a moment, what Martin Buber has called "the injured wholeness of man."*

---

*The context of the phrase runs: "Modern thinkers have undertaken to give a causal explanation of the crisis through various partial aspects: Marx through radical 'alienation' of man caused by the economic and technical revolution, and the psychoanalysts through individual and even collective neuroses. But no one of these attempts at explanation nor all of them together can yield an adequate understanding of what concerns us. We must take the injured wholeness of man upon us as a life burden in order to press beyond all that is merely symptomatic." (*Hasidism and Modern Man*, tr. Maurice Friedman, New York, 1966, p. 38.)

Here, let us remind ourselves, we are dealing with the question of form.

The "made thing" stands as a vital emblem of the integrity of the self, whether the thing is a folk ballad or a high tragedy. But for whom? We never know precisely for whom art is, or on whom, directly or indirectly, it works its effects. But if art turns out to be, in an immediate sense, for only a minority, how can it fortify democracy?

This question usually stirs up a hornet's nest. But to take a few soundings: The fact that all societies have, historically, created art would seem to indicate that it does answer a human need, and that the question is always, or at least up to the present moment, not whether society will have art, but what kind of art it will have. Assuming that man will resist the total transformation that some technologists promise, then it may be pertinent to reflect on the fact that historically a strong and high art is to be associated only with societies of challenging vigor. In such societies ideals of action, creation, and contemplation seem to flower from the same stalk of energy and the same sense of destiny.

Just above I have used the word *associated* in speaking of the relation of strong art to vigorous societies. I have used it because the relation involved remains mysterious; even so, it is hard to believe that either high art or popular art—not "popularized" art, to draw a distinction from the late R. P. Blackmur—is merely an offshoot, a by-product or waste product, that has no significant consequences. It is, rather, an element in a vital dialectic. It is the process by which, in imagining itself and the relation of individuals to one another and to it, a society comes to understand itself, and by understanding, discover its possibilities of growth. Poetry is not, Harry Levin has said, a mere record, but is the "richest and most sensitive of human institutions . . . a rounded organism embracing the people by and for whom it was created."

But how many citizens in our democracy, it will inevitably be asked, are among those "people by and for whom" this rich and sensitive institution has been created? Here we may raise a counterquestion: How many of the institutions that constitute our culture, culture in the broadest sense, does any *one* of us, any particular individual, participate in or understand? For neither question is the test of value a mechanical one: clearly the test is not to count noses for one institution, nor to count the number of institutions involving, directly or indirectly, any particular citizen. The value of an institution lies in the degree in which, by massive or subtle interpenetration and vital relations, that institution combines with others to sustain and foster the individual in his various potentialities, even though any number of such beneficiaries may be unaware of the process.

If we leave this line of thought and turn to the group who are more directly and consciously involved with that "richest and most sensitive of human institutions," something remains to be said to the common charge that poetry—at least "high" poetry—is antidemocratic and encourages elitism. The most obvious thing to say is that poetry, like science, draws not only those who make it but also those who understand and appreciate it, from all sorts of groups, classes, and races. But there is something less obvious and more important to say.

What I am suggesting is that there is a special fluidity in the world of art, and that "elitism" there—if the nasty word be insisted on—is crosshatched with all other kinds of elitism in our democracy. In one sense, it must be granted, the elitism of science (as distinguished from that of technology, which tends to run grain-to-grain with financial elitism) is also crosshatched with the elitisms of our society; the values which "pure" science exhibits in its pursuit of truth are not, in themselves, much prized or richly rewarded in the bustling world of serious concerns. Even so, between the elitism of science and that of art there is a difference, one deriving from the fact that, even to the functionally illiterate, the man in the white jacket pictured in the advertisement holding up a test tube is recognized as a giver—though at second hand, through technology—of practical benefits. The elitism of the arts, however, receives no such acceptance, even at second hand. Its values truly run against the grain of the dominant business-managerial-technological culture; and in this fact it tends to under-cut other elitisms, to work against all the established patterns of prestige. If, as seems probable, the divergence between the arts and the technological society increases, the effect of this special elitism of the arts on social, financial, and technological elitisms will become more marked—and more significant, one is tempted to say, by reason, paradoxically, of its very alienation, for the survival of democracy. Unless certain so-called "democratic" forces have their way, forces that make for a mechanical egalitarianism.

Such forces are numerous, and sometimes even seem to contradict each other; but here let us think of them in general and in relation to the basic notion of democracy in America. Certainly the basis of our democracy is the conviction of the worth of the individual. Democracy does, and should, glorify the "common man." But here comes the rub. The phrase implies two quite distinct and, finally, contradictory meanings.

For the first meaning, let us think of the old Christian notion of the soul of every man as precious in God's sight. But that soul, though precious, was not to be transported automatically to eternal bliss. There was to be prayer, penitence, sweat, pain, works. Even the New England Calvinist, with his doctrine of Election, had to turn his anguished gaze toward a dark inner landscape. What is crucial for the Christian is the will to change, even if the will is futile without God's grace or His Election: and the will to change springs from the love of God—from the adored image of the Good, the Perfect. If we put this into secular terms, we find that the individual soul is precious in the eyes of democracy, but that what is glorified is the *potentiality* in man to become more fully man, more distinctly and strongly a self in fruitful relation to other selves. The qualities that define man as man do not appear in achieved full bloom: man may, for example, be defined as a rational animal, but that does not mean that any particular man may not behave with vicious irrationality. And to continue our translation into secular terms, as the Christian's will to change springs from the love of God, so the will to change in our secular world implies the awareness of standards beyond the easy grasp—perfections that, through love, we may will to approach.

The will to change: this is one of the most precious heritages of American democracy. We have the story of the young Washington, who studied surveying and could, by the exercise of his skill, buy "Bullskin plantation," his first one, at the age of sixteen. Thus far he had merely changed his condition. But he had the will to change himself as well, and with the same furious energy, he studied the Roman Stoics that he might achieve the admirable character he desired. So we have the long list of autodidacts, including Lincoln, Mark Twain, and Dreiser—men who, with all their failings and complications, willed a change deeper than that of an objective condition.

We admire those autodidacts, but the will to change the self is not now deeply characteristic of our democracy. Our glorification of the "common man" more often signifies the notion that the mere fact of commonness in itself constitutes an ideal—and a blessed world it would be in which the actual condition of the self, not the potential, was taken as fulfillment, and in which the ideal coincided so flatteringly with the real, with no pain. Thus, we would live in a perpetual state of redemption without tears, and every man would be, not only King, but God, his own Father, plus being his own Redeemer. In such a world man's function would not be to change himself—for how could Divinity change?— but to change others toward his manifest perfection in the Divine Minimum. The logic of such a world would lead to the dream of Shigalyov, that "fanatic lover of mankind" in *The Possessed*, who dreams a world in which, as Peter Verkhovensky describes it, a "Cicero will have his tongue cut out, Copernicus will have his eyes gouged out, a Shakespeare will be stoned," a world which would "smother every genius in infancy," and "reduce everything to one common denominator."

That world seems a long way off, but it is the world toward which many millions of American citizens, albeit unconsciously, strive. For instance, an eminent lawmaker recently declared that mediocrity is appropriate for the Supreme Court because the mediocre should have their representation. But would he want a surgeon of the Divine Minimum to take out his ailing appendix?

If, however, we are satisfied with the Divine Minimum in ourselves, with no change, we still earnestly desire the Secular Maximum outside. We want the secular millennium, in fact. Man, hard-pressed by the work of the world and eating his bitter bread, has always yearned for the time of liberation. After the War of the Classes is won, Marx promised, there will come a time when man, released from the realm of necessity, can turn to the fulfillment of those capacities that mark him as man—the fulfillment of the potentialities that are common, in varying degrees, to man qua man and that have been thwarted in the era of the bitter bread. But this notion is not special to Marx. It is, in fact, a dream that yet timidly haunts our democratic aspirations and some of the more old-fashioned notions of education.

We have come, inevitably, to the question of work and leisure, and in this connection we should recall the Bible story of the Fall of Man. In Eden, Adam, with Eve, dressed the garden; they were active, not idle, in an activity that fulfilled nature and themselves and was executed in love and piety. In other words, in the Garden, Adam enjoyed leisure, which, as the philosopher Josef Pieper points out, is not idleness but an activity freely chosen and both creative and recreative—an activity in the "preserve of freedom . . . and of that individual humanity which views the world as a whole." And in which, it may be added, the individual may be whole. For in the activity of leisure, as Robert Frost puts it in "Two Tramps in Mud Time," there is the possibility that the avocation and the vocation may combine as do the two eyes to "make one in sight." That is, for the artist, ideally considered, leisure and work are the same, just as it may be said that for the artist means and ends interpenetrate in a process and in an object which finally embodies its own meaning, *is* its own meaning.

To turn back to the myth, Adam, once out of the Garden, was cursed not only by the burden of his impious knowledge of Good and Evil, but by the paradoxical knowledge that, though he was a part of nature (of the earth and now to be returned to the earth), nature had revolted against him to bring forth "thorns and thistles," and that he would henceforth live by the sweat of his brow for his mere bread. He was condemned to live in a realm where work was characteristically of objective necessity—was drudgery, was mere repetitious effort with no choice of ends and little of means. Even in this realm, he might, however, still catch some painful and glorious glimpse of the old activity of the Garden—of the possibility of work as inner fulfillment, an activity in which avocation and vocation might "make one."

Insofar as man could, however imperfectly and fleetingly, recapture a sense of the old activity, it was redemptive in that it relieved him from, first, the curse of existing in a nature turned hostile and, second, of dying into nature. First, by work he might sometimes impose his conception of himself—his self—upon nature in that he humanized his world. Second, what he achieved in this process—object, image, deed, or utterance—gave promise of being durable past his natural span. It was his redemption from death, the Horatian boast: *Non omnis moriar*. It was also a redemption into the fulfilled self.

Redemption from the realm of necessity is what technology promises as the secular millennium. There will be free time for all, uncountable golden hours. But what kind of free time? Free *from* what, and *for* what? Will that time belong to the "preserve of freedom"? Or will the great social problem become, as not a few have suggested, that of maintaining the mental and emotional stability of a pampered and purposeless mass and of lulling it from violence. We may ask why play, sport, social life, and entertainment cannot fill up free time, cannot "kill time" or "pass time," cannot become the new circuses of a people who will have, not only bread, but jam, in plenty. Indeed these activities properly belong to leisure, and do satisfy important human needs. But we are not now speaking of leisure, even in the loosest sense of the word. We are speaking of *free* time, not time free, as now, from some activity that does not characteristically satisfy the natural needs we refer to, but of free time that is free *from* nothing, empty time of infinite duration. Under such conditions would play, sports, entertainment and so on, though necessary, be sufficient for man's well-being? Even now, though they satisfy parts of human nature, they are not adequate to bring man to any sense of the world as a whole and of himself as a whole.

Even if the communal larder does bulge with bread and jam and tickets to all entertainments are free and the Clinic of Aphrodisiacs is open on a twenty-four-hour basis, the new world may, in fact, produce a more drastic fragmentation of man than we now endure. In the cybernetic paradise some work will still be needed, but work appropriate only for citizens of high intelligence and special training; and so, in a comic inversion of history, all work may become a privilege reserved for the elite. Only the elite, in that new meritocracy, would enjoy the opportunity for self-fulfillment in significant effort, in free choice of ends and means in a project conceived of in a medium of "real" time, and not in an eternal, self-devouring present of successive stimuli. The elite, then, would exclusively have the opportunity for pursuing the ideal of the wholeness of man, and for viewing the world as a whole. And so we would be back where we started, in the old world before the advent of technology, with a tiny island of leisure (work-as-leisure) afloat in a vast sea, not of work as drudgery, but of drugged boredom.

We may well be moving toward the secular millennium of free time, but can we convert that free time into something approaching the ideal of leisure? Can we use that time for activity freely chosen because, no matter what other rewards it may bring (and it should bring other rewards, as well), it is an activity fulfilling the doer in the doing? Certainly there is a capacity and need in human nature that would allow us to think of free time as being used to some significant degree in activities which approach the nature of poetry, of art.

I am not suggesting that in an ideal use of free time a man would take up finger painting or raffia work. What I do suggest is that art obviously provides the most perfect example of self-fulfilling activity, the kind of activity of which gratuitous joy in the way of the doing is the mark, and in which the doer pursues the doing as a projection of his own nature upon objective nature, thereby discovering both the law of the medium in which he chooses to work and his own nature. A man need not create art in order to participate, with varying degrees of consciousness, in the order of experience from which art flows, but it is hard to believe that, in the mysterious texture of things, a world in which art does not find a place would ever long harbor men who find, in some degree, intrinsic significance in the process of life.

Nothing that I have said is intended to imply that the practice of art, any more than the appreciation of it, is to be thought of as, intrinsically, either self-indulgence or self-help. Art can thrive only insofar as the practitioner or appreciator looks beyond himself and assumes some standard for the thing made. The nature of such a standard, it must be emphasized, is special. Unlike the standard of the manufacturer or, even, craftsman, that of the artist is not externally proposed;

it is the artist's painful and distinguishing task to discover, in the very process of creating each particular work, the standard itself.

And this sense of standard applies to popular as well as to high art. It is "popularized" art, art as mere commodity, that, in its lack of standards and its glorification of easy and stereotyped availability, is the enemy of distinction. And of *distinctions*. For the making of distinctions in the nature of experience, in the nature of life as lived, is at the center of any art. And of any life that is not, to use the Socratic term, "uninspected."

There are indications that we may be moving toward a sense of true leisure, and there is no inherent reason why technology, in addition to creating free time, may not be a force toward converting free time into leisure. But let us not shut our eyes to certain aspects of American free time as it now exists. Just as it is largely characterized by compulsive consumption, it is characterized by passivity. Spectacle as well as goods may be merely consumed. The non-participating viewer is a "consumer." He tends to have no stake in events except one artificially created, as by a bet or by some stipulated commitment of the ego. At the best he is a "fan," and what we have in our society is the general psychology of the fan, which implies a diminution of the true self by the creation of a fictively inflated self. Even events in the news, world-shaking events sometimes, wind up as mere spectacle, with cynical detachment—finally political and social alienation—as the inevitable result of merely artificial commitment.

We have lately seen what may yet turn into an example of such cynical detachment. After two years of our exfoliating national scandals, the newspapers began to air their own concern that the public was getting bored. They feared that the great overarching and undergirding significance of the events reported might be little in the face of the fact that the news was not keeping "new" enough, was not amusing, diverting, surprising, sensational. If knowledge of the public resides anywhere, it should reside in the newspaper offices, and if this time they turn out to be wrong, the fact, however cheering, is no guarantee that they will be wrong about the general drift of things. In any case, in a world of the eternal present, in which passivity is fed by a progressively intense diet of sensation and novelty, significance, which necessarily refers to the past and the future, is not significant.

In this passivity, which is indeed a sad index of the sense of relief from necessity, we find, however, that energy does persist; but this energy, since it finds no significant outlet, tends to degenerate into violence, often in the strange marriage of pathology and ideology so characteristic of our moment. Again, when energy does flag, we observe the obsessive quest for violent stimulation in much the same way as pornography inevitably tends toward perversion. Man, as Veblen once remarked, has an innate "repugnance to all futility of effort," and must create false meaning when true meaning is not available. Interest assumes the possibility of meaning, but excitement may—and excitement as mere stimulation always does—move toward futility. And man's last reaction to this entrapment in futility, which denies the responsible self, may well be self-denigration or self-hatred, which more and more appears as a theme in our literature: hero as slob. For in our society the true hero is, if not dead, very sick. We have, in his place, the "celebrity." And the celebrity is, of course, the hero of the "de-selfed" man—and of the public of "non-selves."

I have been speaking of the passivity characteristic of our current notion of free time. As a last irony, let us turn to the words so frequently uttered by the yearning young—and, as a special phenomenon of our time, by the yearning not quite old, as well: "I am going to take time off and find myself." "Time off" from school, from job, from wife—from what? Free time: "to get away from it all"—whatever "all" is. But the key phrase is "to find myself."

In the phrase lurks the idea that the self is a pre-existing entity, a self like a Platonic idea existing in a mystic realm beyond time and change. No, rather an object like the nugget of gold in the placer pan, the Easter egg under the bush at an Easter-egg hunt, a four-leaf clover to promise miraculous luck. Here is the essence of passivity, to think to find, by luck, one's quintessential luck. And the essence of absurdity, too, for the self is never to be found, but must be created, not the happy accident of passivity, but the product of a thousand actions, large and small, conscious or unconscious, performed not "away from it all," but in the face of "it all," for better or for worse, in work and leisure rather than in free time. If, echoing Buffon's old saying, we declare that style is the man, then with equal justice, we may declare that the self is a style of being, continually expanding in a vital process of definition, affirmation, revision, and growth, a process that is the image, we may say, of the life process of a healthy society itself.

To sum up our general ideas of the relation of free time and the self, we may adapt the formulation framed long ago by Stuart Chase that leisure, which should offer *re-creation*, has become for numberless people *de-creation*. What, in a good world, would be created in the process of work would be a self, and in such a world, what would be "re-created" in leisure would be, by the same token, a self. What all too often happens, in the free time of our not so very good world, is that what self may persist is, actually, "de-created."

But how does poetry come into all this? By being an antidote, a sovereign antidote, for passivity. For the basic fact about poetry is that it demands participation, from the secret physical echo in muscle and nerve that identifies us with the medium, to the imaginative enactment that stirs the deepest recesses where life-will and values reside. Beyond that, it nourishes our life-will in the process of testing our values. And this is not to be taken as implying a utilitarian aesthetic. It is, rather, one way of describing our pleasure in poetry as an adventure in the celebration of life.

Where does this leave us?

We, in the flush of pride in technological prowess, may be like Melville's Ahab, who, in a blaze of self-knowledge as he drove the *Pequod* toward catastrophe, exclaimed: "All my means are sane; my motive and object mad!" But what may bring us to our senses? And whether by disaster, luck, or a sudden access of wisdom, what kind of sense can we come to?

Will the conditioned man—the happy, programmed robot, the hero of the Technetronic Age—take over—with all bets then off, of course? Or will the technological order, though short of the cybernetic paradise, persist, with enough new and glittering triumphs to reduce dissent to a harmless minority? Or do we face the imminent collapse of the human project as we have known it? Or can the collapse be avoided by the development of some technology, or even science, "of limits"? Or will the technological and humanistic orders achieve some sort of interpenetration, an unpredictable osmosis, so that a pansacramentalism of the sort Buber discusses may emerge? In any case, great changes are indeed taking place, and Buber has, perhaps, given the most fundamental definition of this "something" that is "slowly evolving in the human soul." It is, he says, "the most intimate of all resistances—resistance to mass or collective loneliness," a loneliness that Vico long ago described as coming at a late phase of civilization, when men, "no matter how great the throng and press of their bodies, live like wild beasts in a deep solitude of spirit and will," and when the sense of community withers as each man seeks to follow only his "own pleasure or caprice."

It is sentimental, however, to try to retrace our steps, to try to demote science, the purest expression of the love of intellectual beauty, to the role of a scullery maid or to deny the special, and in an economic sense primary, role of technology. And I flinch, also, from those who, like Henry James, would assume art to be the justification of all life, as well as from all others—among them a number of our self-appointed liberators—who refuse to recognize the hard costs of mere survival for many millions of human beings, the cost in grinding effort and irremediable pain. How can anybody who has lived through the Great Depression, or even walked through parts of Appalachia or a slum, feel otherwise?

I must confess that I flinch, too, from the view of W. H. Auden, that splendid poet, who, in an essay on Yeats, implies that art is merely a "product of history" and, unlike other products, such as technical inventions, never a "cause," an "effective agent"; and who adds that, "if not a poem had been written, not a picture painted, not a bar of music composed, the history of man would be materially unchanged." This strikes me as, simply, bad psychology: the notion that the human psyche can be regarded as divisible into airtight compartments. It would seem that, granting the existence of an aesthetic value distinguishable from other aspects of experience, this value has both its origins in, and its effects on, the massive texture of human needs and human life. Can we totally separate the "material" world, as Auden here does, from what we may call, generally, the "spiritual" world? Even if the tendency to make such a separation is an aspect of the self-destructive drive of our culture? Or, to approach the whole question from another angle, can it be said that the arts offer us no knowledge, that all knowledge must come to us from science?

No, Auden's view is too much like what Gibbon, speaking from the ironical wisdom of the Enlightenment, said: "Among a polished people poetry is rather an amusement of the fancy than a passion of the soul." I suppose that I do think of poetry as, if not a passion of the soul, then the voice of the passion of the soul—though that lingo is high falutin. Even a nourishment of the soul, and indeed of society, in that it keeps alive the sense of self and the correlated sense of a community.

Poetry even, in the same act and the same moment, helps one to grasp reality and to grasp one's own life. Not that it will give definitions and certainties. But it can help us to ponder on what Saint Augustine meant when he said that he was a question to himself.

Behind such a question, there lies our divided nature.

There is the self of appetite and action, and the self that observes and ponders appetite and action. I suppose I see life, for all our yearning for and struggle toward primal or supernal unity of being, as a more or less oscillating process. On that day when the hairless ape felt the first flicker of self-consciousness and self-criticism, and was first aware that something inside him was looking at something else inside him, he was doomed, as we are doomed, to live, both in the flesh and in society, in the bright irony and long anguish of the machine and the vision—for that is what we are, machines capable of vision. But we, even though we are machines and even for the true good offered to us by machines that we have created, cannot afford to let the faculty of vision blur. And how much less can we afford it for the specious good!

We cannot afford it, for we must live by distinctions. And we may say that poetry provides, to come back to our earlier terms, the Archimedean point from which we can make distinctions, from which we can consider the world of technology and, indeed, of democracy. And to consider, of course, the world of the self. For if once the oscillation, the vibrance, the dialectic ceases, life, as we know it and esteem it, will cease. Then, to quote the end of Pope's *Dunciad*:

Thy Hand, Great Anarch! let the curtain fall;
And Universal Darkness buries All.

We are not, however, for all our dunce-ness, necessarily condemned to that—even if process may be thought to be all, even if there is to be no millennium of any kind. As a last word, I'll quote again from the *Confessions* of Saint Augustine:

There is a dim glimmering of light unput-out in men; let them walk, let them walk that the darkness overtake them not.

Notes

Notes

ii St.-John Perse, "And it is enough": "On Poetry," Speech of Acceptance upon the Award of the Nobel Prize for Literature, December 10, 1960; translated by W. H. Auden.

5 Emerson, "Leave this hypocritical prating": "Considerations by the Way," *The Conduct of Life*, Boston, 1903, p. 237.

6 Cooper "defective systems": *cit.* Robert F. Spiller, *Fenimore Cooper*, New York, 1931, p. 315.

6-7 Cooper, "as soon as the money-getting principle": *The Ways of the Hour*, New York, 1851, p. 49.

7 Cooper, "democratic gentleman": *The American Democrat*, New York, 1956, p. 95.

8 Thoreau (a) "any man more right": "Civil Disobedience," *Walden and Other Writings*, ed. Brooks Atkinson, New York, 1937, p. 647; (b) "dirty institutions": *ibid.*, p. 155.

9 Henry Adams (a) "my philosophy teaches": Letter to Charles Francis Adams, Jr., October 2, 1863, *A Cycle of Adams Letters*, ed. Worthington Chauncey Ford, Boston, 1926, II, 90; (b) "great principle of democracy": May 1, 1863, *ibid.*, I, 282.

10 Holmes (a) "all life is an experiment": "Abrams v. United States," *The Mind and Faith of Justice Holmes*, ed. Max Lerner, New York, 1943, p. 312; (b) "cosmic ganglion": Letter of April

2, 1926, *Holmes-Pollock Letters*, ed. Mark DeWolfe Howe, Cambridge, Mass., 1941, II, 178; (c) "predatory animal," "death of men": Letter of February 1, 1920, *ibid.*, II, 36.

11 Holmes "I loathe the thick-fingered": *cit.* Mark DeWolfe Howe, *Oliver Wendell Holmes: The Shaping Years, 1841-1870*, Cambridge, Mass., 1957, p. 140.

12 Adams, Jr., "The great operations of": "An Erie Raid," *North American Review*, April 1871, p. 241.

12 Vanderbilt, "You can't keep such": *New York Times*, August 30, 1879.

13 Emerson, "Money . . . is in its effects": "Nominalist and Realist," *Essays, Second Series*, Boston, 1903, p. 231.

13 Bishop William Lawrence, "Godliness is in league": "The Relation of Wealth to Morals," *World's Work*, New York, 1900, pp. 287-290.

15 Howells, "A great cycle": Kenneth S. Lynn: "Howells in the Nineties," *Visions of America*, Westport, Conn., 1973, p. 78.

16 Rosenberg: "Revolution and the Idea of Beauty," *Encounter*, December 1953, p. 65.

16 Yeats: "We make out of the quarrel with others, rhetoric, but of the quarrel with ourselves, poetry" in "Anima Hominis," *Per Silentia Lunae*, in *Essays*, New York, 1924, p. 492.

17 Twain (a) "As to the past": Letter to Will Bowen, August 31, 1876, *Mark Twain's Letters to Will Bowen*, ed. Theodore Hornberger, Austin, 1941, pp. 23-24; (b) "simply a hymn": *cit.* E. Wagenknecht, *Mark Twain: The Man and His World*, New Haven, 1935, p. 66; (c) "money-getting": *cit.* Justin Kaplan, *Mr. Clemens and Mark Twain*, New York, 1966, p. 99; (d) "All I wish to urge you": "An Open Letter to Commodore Vanderbilt," *Packard's Monthly Magazine*, March 1869.

21 Twain (a) "if it were only to write": Letter of September 22, 1889, *The Writings of Mark Twain*, ed. E. B. Paine, New

York, 1929, XXXV, 514; (b) "The Great Republic was": *Letters from the Earth*, ed. Bernard DeVoto, New York, 1926, p. 109.

22 Twain, "I dreamed I was born": Letter of March 19, 1893, *cit*. G. C. Bellamy, *Mark Twain As a Literary Artist*, Norman, 1950, p. 365.

23 Lynn: *The Dream of Success: A Study of the Modern American Imagination*, Boston, 1955, pp. 28-35.

28 Faulkner, "had the gift of living once": New York, 1936, p. 89.

36 Conversation between former President Nixon and H. R. Haldeman, June 23, 1972, as reported in the *New York Times* reprint of the White House transcripts, August 8, 1974, p. 15.

36 Buber, "the most intimate of all": "The Utopian Element in Socialism," *Paths in Utopia*, tr. R. F. C. Hull, New York, 1950, p. 15.

41 "it is now trivial to say": Daniel Callahan, *The Tyranny of Survival*, New York, 1973, p. 23.

42-43 Brzezinski, "Can the institutions of political democracy": "America in the Technetronic Age," *Encounter*, January 1968, p. 20.

43 Dubos, aggressive technology: *Essays in Honor of David Lyall Patrick*, Tucson, 1971, pp. 6-7.

45 Erikson, "a species mortally dangerous": *Dimensions of a New Identity*, New York, 1974, p. 31.

46 "We regard *men* as infinitely": *cit*. Massimo Teodori, *The New Left*, Indianapolis, 1969, p. 116.

47-48 Vico, "chaotic visions": *The New Science*, tr. T. G. Bergin and M. H. Fisch, New York, 1961, pp. xxxvi, xl, xlix, 52-53, 57-63; and Bendetto Croce, *The Philosophy of Giambattista Vico*, tr. R. G. Collingwood, New York, 1913, pp. 1-72.

48 Kierkegaard: *A Kierkegaard Anthology*, ed. Robert Walter Bretall, New York, 1946, pp. 214-215.

48 Russell: *The Scientific Outlook*, New York, 1931, pp. 260-269.

49 Yeats, "Descartes, Locke, and": Diary entry, September 15, 1930, *Explorations*, New York, 1962, p. 325.

51 Whitehead, "if civilization is to survive": *Modes of Throught*, New York, 1931, p. 63.

51 Sinnott, "teleology, far from being": *Matter, Mind and Man*, New York, 1957, p. 42.

53 Santayana, "no transcendental logic": "The Genteel Tradition in American Philosophy," *Winds of Doctrine and Platonism and the Spiritual Life*, New York, 1957, p. 213.

55 Plumb, "as the interpreter of men's": Boston, 1970, p. 138.

57 Buber: *I and Thou*, tr. Walter Kaufman, New York, 1970, pp. 84-89.

57-58 Ellul, "phenomenon of technical convergence": *The Technical Society*, tr. John Wilkinson, New York, 1967, p. 391.

60 Boorstin: *The Image: or What Became of the American Dream*, New York, 1962.

61 Kierkegaard, "body that can never be reviewed": *A Kierkegaard Anthology*, pp. 265-266.

65 Marx, "truth is without passion": *cit.* Stanley Edgar Hyman, *The Tangled Bank—Darwin, Marx, Frazier and Freud as Imaginative Writers*, New York, 1962, pp. 111-112. (In the context, it seems, Hyman implies that the quotation is from *The Eighteenth Brumaire*, but I do not find it there.)

65 Baudelaire: ed. Charles Du Bos, Paris, 1930, p. 172.

65 Jung: *The Undiscovered Self*, tr. R. F. C. Hull, Boston, 1958, pp. 13-14.

66 Engels, "has subdued the forces of nature": "On Authority," *Marx and Engels: Basic Writings on Politics and Philosophy*, ed. Lewis Feuer, New York, 1959, p. 483.

69 Jung, "Resistance to the organized mass": *The Undiscovered Self*, p. 60 (italics in text).

71 Bergson, "into our own presence": *Time and Free Will: an Essay On the Immediate Data of Consciousness*, tr. F. L. Pogson,

London, 1910, p. 134.

72 Nietzsche, "enchantment": *The Birth of Tragedy*, tr. Francis Golffing, New York, 1956, p. 56.

73 Williams, "No ideas but": *Paterson*, New York, 1963, p. 9.

73 Klee, not to reflect but: "Opinions on Creation," *Paul Klee*, New York, 1946, pp. 10 ff.

73. Conrad, "Before all, to": *Nigger of the Narcissus*, London, 1897, p. x.

75 Blackmur, "popularized" art: "Chaos Is Come Again, *Southern Review*, Spring 1941, pp. 660-661.

76 Levin: "Memoirs of Scholars: Milman Parry," *Grounds for Comparison*, Cambridge, Mass., 1942, p. 143.

80 Dostoievski: "Cicero will have his tongue": part II, ch. 8.

81 Pieper, "preserve of freedom": *Leisure, the Basis of Culture*, tr. Alexander Dru, New York, 1964, p. 33.

83 Horace: *Odes*, book III, xxx.

88 Veblen, "repugnance to all futility of effort": *The Theory of the Leisure Class*, New York, 1934, p. 33.

88 "celebrity": Boorstin, *The Image*, pp. 45-76.

89 Chase, for numberless people *decreation: Men and Machines*, New York, 1930, pp. 256 ff.

90-91 Buber, "slowly evolving in the human soul": *Paths in Utopia*, Boston, 1958, p. 15.

91 Vico, "no matter how great the throng": *The New Science*, p. 381.

91 Auden, "product of history": "The Public v. the Late Mr. William Butler Yeats," *Partisan Review*, Spring 1939, p. 51.

92 Gibbon, "Among a polished people": *The History of the Decline and Fall of the Roman Empire*, London, 1926, I, 249.

92 Augustine, a question to himself: tr. William Watts, New York, 1926, book x, ch. xxxiii, p. 168.

94 Augustine, "There is a dim glimmering": *ibid.*, book x, ch. xxiii, p. 137.

CREDITS

I thank the following for permission to quote:

Harper & Row—for the passage from "Papers of the Adam Family"; quoted on page 21. From Mark Twain, *Letters from the Earth*, edited by Bernard DeVoto, New York, Harper & Row, 1926.

Mark Twain Memorial, Hartford, Connecticut—for a passage from the letter from Samuel L. Clemens to Sue Crane, March 19, 1893; quoted on page 22.

Viking Press—for four lines from "The Triumph of the Machine"; quoted on page 44. From *The Complete Poems of D. H. Lawrence*, edited by Vivian de Sola Pinto and Warren Roberts, copyright 1964 and 1971 by Angelo Ravagli and C. M. Weekly, Executors of the Estate of Frieda Lawrence Ravagli. All rights reserved. Reprinted by permission of The Viking Press, Inc.

Macmillan—for two lines from "Two Songs from a Play"; quoted.on page 50. From *Collected Poems of William Butler Yeats*, copyright 1928, by Macmillan Publishing, Inc.; renewed 1956 by Georgie Yeats.

Random House—for the first four lines from "The Unknown Citizen"; quoted on page 61. Copyright 1940 and renewed 1968 by W. H. Auden. Reprinted from W. H. Auden, *Collected Shorter Poems, 1927-1957*, by permission of Random House, Inc.

Harvard University Press—for the lines from Augustine; quoted on page 94. From *Confessions*, book X, ch. xxiii; translated by W. Watts, Loeb Library edition, Cambridge, Massachusetts, 1912.

Parts of the Jefferson Lecture have appeared in *The Southern Review* and the *New York Review of Books*.